*To Dom,
Blessed Christmas
to you - all year long.*

Energies

Material, Vital, Cosmic

*With Gratitude,
Anthony Colibrando*

Other books by John G. Bennett

A Spiritual Psychology
Creative Thinking
Deeper Man
Gurdjieff: A Very Great Enigma
Gurdjieff: Making a New World
How We Do Things: The Role of Attention
in Spiritual Life
Is There "Life" on Earth?
Long Pilgrimage
Sacred Influences
Talks on Beelzebub's Tales
The Dramatic Universe
Vol 1 The Foundations of Natural Philosophy
Vol 2 The Foundations of Moral Philosophy
Vol 3 Man and His Nature
Vol 4 History
The Masters of Wisdom
The Sevenfold Work
The Way To Be Free
Transformation
Witness: An Autobiography

Energies

Material, Vital, Cosmic

John G. Bennett

Claymont Communications
Charles Town, West Virginia

First published in 1964 by Coombe Springs Press

ISBN 0-934254-27-3 cloth
0-934254-28-1 paper

Cover illustration: Five Dreamings, 1984, by Michael Nelson
Jakamarra, assisted by Marjorie Napaljarri, Papunyu, Central
Australia. Acrylic on canvas, 122 x 182 cm. Photograph by
Michael Kluvanek for the South Australia Museum. Used by
permission of the Aboriginal Artists' Agency, 12 McLaren Street,
North Sydney, Australia 2060; with thanks to The Asia Society,
New York, New York.

Library of Congress Cataloguing-in-Publication Data

Bennett, John G. 1897-1974.
Energies.
1. Force and energy. 2. Vital force. 3. Life. 4. Bennett, John G.
Dramatic Universe. I. Title.
B1618.B43E5   1989   89-891 CIP

Contents

Foreword   Page   i

Preface   v

LECTURE I   The Twelve Kinds of Energy   1

LECTURE II   The Transformations of Energy   25

LECTURE III   How Energies Do Their Work   49

LECTURE IV   The Secret of Creativity   73

LECTURE V   The Last Question   91

POSTSCRIPT   The Works Of Love   117

Foreword

J OHN G. BENNETT (1897-1974), a man of exceptional insight
  and accomplishment, devoted his life to seeking the meaning of
human existence. He traveled extensively in Asia in the early
years of this century, intially as an officer and interpreter for
British Military Intelligence. His skills as a linguist — he spoke six
languages fluently, and several dialects of Central Asia — opened
doors for him, and he was able to make contact with many
prominent spiritual and political leaders. He returned to the East
again and again, convinced that the keys to spiritual transformation lay in the wisdom of the ancient teachings. In 1920, while in
Turkey, he met G. I. Gurdjieff whose work, and his central
question, "What is the sense and significance of life on the Earth,
and human life in particular?" became a touchstone for Bennett's
search. After a period of work with Gurdjieff at Fontainebleau,
Bennett returned to England, where he studied with Gurdjieff's
student P. D. Ouspensky for several years, while developing his
career as a scientist in industrial research. After the Second World
War, Bennett was reunited with Gurdjieff in Paris and entered an
intensive period of personal work with him, which came to an end
with Gurdjieff's death in 1949. Although he continued to explore
other traditions, Bennett regarded Gurdjieff as his teacher
throughout his life.

A brilliant scientist and mathematician, Bennett brought a
trained intellect to his spiritual search; the result was a powerful

synthesis — a comprehensive, practical approach to transformation. Gifted with an uncommon ability to transmit his understanding to others, Bennett worked with students both individually and in groups over nearly five decades, maintaining an attitude of search and research, of experimentation and question. In 1964, he founded the Institute for the Comparative Study of History, Philosophy and the Sciences; the Institute's property, Coombe Springs, in England, became a well-known center for group work, seminars, and study. Bennett spoke of continuous education, and referred to his life as a "work in progress." In his teaching, he elucidated the relationship between knowledge, being, and will — that ideas must penetrate beyond the intellect to reach a deeper part of us, and that knowledge must be amplified by awareness. In his exploration of the religious and devotional, he delved deeply into traditional rituals, seeking the common spiritual action at their roots.

Bennett developed a scale of energies and their transformations, in which he intended to present many of the ideas from Gurdjieff's *All & Everything* in a form that was easier to grasp. He sought an essential understanding of the path we travel when we enter into the spiritual worlds. His studies on universal energies, which took place in the 1950's, describe spirituality as energy, occurring on a finer level than our ordinary experience. Each spiritual action has its own unique quality of energy, which is its contribution to the cosmic process. Man is part of and participates in this spectrum of energies, and his evolutionary path lies in choosing to participate consciously in the refinement of energies. Through struggle with oneself, and a deep, objective seeing of our situation as it is, certain intermediate energies are produced, which allows help to come from a higher level.

> It is not enough to have the good will to do it; it is also necessary to have new kinds of perception, new understandings . . . Therefore we have also the obligation to understand life better, and this starts with understanding what human life is for and how this something is to be produced through the way we live our lives. [1]

ii

Seeing the disintegration of values in contemporary culture, the neglect of the needs of the planet, and the alienation of the individual as symptoms of a spiritual crisis, Bennett taught the necessity of cooperation between man, nature, and the higher powers. In presenting this view of personal evolution in a cosmic context, and in his work to prepare others to serve the needs of the future, Bennett went beyond despair to the hope inherent in "work on oneself."

> The answer to the question that Gurdjieff himself proposed . . . is that human life is required to produce something that is needed for the harmony of the solar system, and particularly for this planet . . . this something is produced by the way we live our lives and the way we die our deaths . . . Man is not intended just to live for his own egoistic purposes; he has obligations to fulfill . . . and in fulfilling these can fulfill himself. This is the notion of the transformation of man. [2]

In 1971, drawing on fifty years of practice and experience, Bennett undertook a ten-month residential program at the International Academy for Continuous Education at Sherborne House in England, where people from all parts of the world gathered to learn and live the techniques of transformation. Shortly before his death in 1974, Claymont Court, in West Virginia, was purchased, where an experiment in intentional community, based on methods of inner work, was begun.

Bennett's life work ranged from a study of the entire body of human knowledge and understanding (*The Dramatic Universe*) to the power of a moment of attention in an individual life. *Energies, How We Do Things,* and *Creative Thinking* were compiled by Bennett, based on lectures he gave during the late 1950's and early 1960's. We are re-issuing these books now to give the reader a taste of the extraordinary vision and practice that emerged from his lifelong search.

[1]From an unpublished talk by J. G. Bennett in 1973.
[2]Ibid.

Preface

THESE LECTURES WERE GIVEN IN 1956, when I had just completed one of the periodical revisions of *The Dramatic Universe*[1], and were an attempt to explain in simple language the theory of energies developed in Chapter 32 of that work. They happened to coincide with my first experience of Subud and the discerning reader will recognize passages that refer to this experience.

They are being published almost as they were given, not because I would express myself in exactly the same terms today; but because I can see how useful it is to have a broad grasp of the nature of energy and its various qualities. There is a valid sense in which it can be said that nothing is more important for us than to understand about energies, for our destiny depends upon our ability to make right use of the energies available to us. This right use can be achieved by "right conduct" without understanding what we are doing — much as a cook can make a good meal with no understanding of the principles of nutrition and biochemistry. Unfortunately, the rules of right conduct can never be either precise or comprehensive enough to ensure that we shall make right use of our energies in all circumstances. Still more unfortunately, the circumstances which defy guidance by rules are not always trivial. Some of the most important occasions are unique and arrive so unexpectedly that we cannot prepare for them. To find the right action in such cases we need to understand what is happening to us; and that, very often, means to be able to distinguish between one kind of energy and another.

Again, the use of energies is a highly technical matter. We know this well enough in dealing with nuclear energy or even the more accessible energies of electricity, heat, and motion. We do not expect to drive a car by the light of nature, or to build an electrical generator without any knowledge of electrical engineering.

The vital energies are round us and in us and our very existence depends upon their use. The ordinary satisfactions of life depend upon transformations of energy. The control of these transformations is a highly technical matter. When it goes wrong, we are sick and send for the doctor — but right use is far more than the avoidance of illness. The capacity for work and enjoyment depends upon the availability of the right energies in the right place — and how little we know of the techniques required.

Our deeper well-being — in the psychological sense — depends upon energies of another kind; but they are still energies and their control and use is pre-eminently a technical matter. Nearly all the emotional and mental suffering to which mankind is subject is due to the failure to use psychic energies rightly. This is obvious to all in the case of the sexual energy; but it is no less true for the energies of thought and feeling. Psychology is scarcely at the threshold of the understanding of psychic energies. Gurdjieff knew more of the techniques involved than anyone else I have met or heard of. He taught us many of these techniques in the form of exercises and disciplines. He went further and set up a scheme of energies — or as he called them "substances" — that was the starting point of my own investigations. Students of Gurdjieff's ideas will recognize in the present book many of the notions contained in the chapter "Purgatory" of *Beelzebub's Tales to His Grandson*[2]; though, I hope, in a form that is easier to grasp.

Finally, there is the role of energies in the transformation of man himself. Gurdjieff defined man as a "cosmic apparatus for the transformation of energy." Man's being and also his becoming, his

vi

actual existence and his potentiality for attaining to a fuller or higher life, equally depend upon transformations of energy. These transformations fall into three categories. First of all, there are the transformations which are or ought to be under man's own control. Secondly, there are those that depend upon his cooperation or submission, but can neither be initiated nor maintained by an action of his own. Thirdly, there are transformations that are wholly beyond man's power to understand or to direct.

These three transformations correspond to the three main elements in the spiritual life of man. The first is the element of understanding and "work upon oneself," of which Gurdjieff was one of the foremost exponents in our time. The second action, which is that of submission, is particularly well exemplified in the Subud *latihan*. The nature of this action is that it requires from man consent and submission, but no work of his own. The third kind of transformation is properly to be called "supernatural." It is sacramental in character because man can participate in it only through an external act, but without any consciousness of its true character. This third kind of action belongs to the religious life, but it is none the less a transformation of energies. It is abundantly clear that the Sacraments of the Christian religion do concern supernatural energy transformations. This is true of all the Sacraments from Baptism through the Eucharist to the Last Unction.

If, then, transformations of energy concern us in every phase of our lives, we should be wise to do everything in our power to understand energies better. It is not enough to do this theoretically, for energies are primarily for use and only secondarily for knowledge. This is as true of the psychic and spiritual energies as it is for the physical and vital energies.

In this book, I show how energies can best be studied according to twelve great qualities, within each of which there are various kinds and intensities. Within this range, four energies are of direct significance for our human experience. These are the energies that operate in our conscious life, and which we can to some extent control or regulate. I have called them the automatic,

sensitive, conscious, and creative energies. A practical understanding of these four energies enables a man to regulate his own
life upon almost all the levels of experience open to him. Nevertheless, to grasp their full significance, one should see them
within the total structure of energies from the material to the
cosmic.

Coombe Springs
June 1964

[1]J. G. Bennett, *The Dramatic Universe*, Volumes I-IV, Claymont Communications
(Charles Town, West Virginia: 1987).
[2]G. I. Gurdjieff, *Beelzebub's Tales to His Grandson*, E. P. Dutton (New York: 1973).

LECTURE I

The Twelve Kinds of Energy

WHY DO WE WANT TO STUDY ENERGIES? It is because everything that is done in us and in the whole world is done through the transformations of energy. Therefore, if we want to learn how to do anything, large or small, what we are really learning is how to use energies. Most of the time, we have no idea that this is what we are doing, any more than a baby learning to walk realizes that it is learning how to use energy. But there are some processes that can be directed intentionally only if one understands what has to be done with energies. And this can be very important for us. Our aim should be that ultimately we shall be able to direct our own work, and not always depend upon being told what to do; we can be helped towards this if we can understand for ourselves something about energies and their transformations.

WHAT IS ENERGY?

In the ordinary schoolbook teaching of mechanics, energy is defined as the **power to do work**. Here, only mechanical work is referred to, but the same definition can be applied to energies that have nothing to do with ordinary mechanics. Whatever kind of

1

work we have to do, we need the corresponding kind of energy in order to do it. And it has to be the **corresponding**, or right kind, of energy. For example, if I want my watch to go, I have to wind up the spring. That means I put some energy into the spring and then the watch will go. I cannot use any other kind of energy for winding the watch. If I want to cook an egg, I have to boil water — but it is no use putting my watch on the gas stove to get it wound up. If I want my car to go, I have to put the energy obtained from the burning petrol into it. If I want my body to go, I have to put the energy from food into it — but I cannot put food into my car and I cannot feed myself on petrol.

It is just the same with our psychic functions. Each kind of inner work requires energy of a particular quality. Let us say we want to feel: there is a particular quality of energy which is necessary in order to feel in a particular sensitive way that goes beyond our habitual automatic reactions. We may be aware of the difference, but not realize what is required. The result will be that we shall find that our reactions are not at all what we intend. If we use the energy which is quite sufficient for our automatic functioning — automatic seeing, automatic mental associations — and try to feel with it, our feelings will not go, any more than the watch will go if I put it on the gas stove. So, energy is the power to do work, but each kind of work requires the appropriate kind of energy.

THE CHARACTERISTICS OF ENERGY

We have just seen that there are different kinds, different qualities, of energy, and for every kind of work a particular quality is needed. But energies do not differ only in **quality**, they also differ in two other ways: in **quantity** and in **intensity**. In order to determine the energy that is available or required for a particular kind of work, we have to know three different things: first, what quality of energy we have to use; second, what is the quantity; and third, what is its intensity.

INTENSITY

Just to help you to see what I mean by these three kinds of things, let us talk again about **heat**. I want to boil an egg. I know that heat is the kind of energy I need for this. So, already — from my ordinary experience of life — I recognize that there is one particular quality of energy I need to cook an egg, and I do not expect to use some other quality. But I also know that there is a certain intensity required. By intensity of heat, I mean what is usually called the **temperature**. For example, I know that warm water will not coagulate the albumen, or as we say, "cook" it. The water has to be at a certain temperature, and that means at the certain intensity called "boiling." If it is much more intense than that, it will only dry up the egg or even burn it to a cinder. But supposing that I want to melt iron: it is no use putting a bar of iron into boiling water — it will not melt. So we see that the intensity which is quite sufficient to cook an egg, is not sufficient to melt iron. It has to be much hotter — more than red hot, in fact — white hot. And when we speak about "red hot" and "white hot" we are using expressions which convey our recognition that there are different intensities of heat.

QUANTITY

Energy is not a matter of intensity only, but also of quantity. We know that if the gas pressure is very bad, it will take a long time for water to boil. Or if we have a very tiny flame, like a match, we will never get our water to boil at all. We understand very well that there is such a thing as quantity of heat because that is what we pay for. We pay for our gas in so many pennies a therm, or for our coal in so many pounds a ton; and what we are paying for is **quantity**.

USE

The intensity we get out of energy to some extent depends on us, on the way we use it. If we use the right mixture of gas and air, we get a hot flame; if we use too much gas or too much air, we cannot get the highest possible temperature. There are always these three properties — quality, intensity, and quantity — in any kind of energy with which we have to deal. It is just the same with electrical energy. Electrical energy can easily be turned into other qualities, so that we sometimes forget that electrical energy itself is neither hot nor able to make wheels turn around, but has to pass through some apparatus for that. Electrical energy has a certain quality of its own which is quite different from that of the other kinds of energy. It has intensity which we call electromotive force, which we usually measure as "voltage." If we want to get a great big spark, we know that we have to use a very high voltage. We look at lightning coming from the clouds, and we know that perhaps millions of volts are required in order to break down the resistance between the cloud and the earth, while only a few volts are sufficient to make a lamp burn brightly. We also know very well from experience of our ordinary practice in buying electricity that it also has quantity measured in electrical units, such as "kilowatt-hours."

So, we could go through all the different kinds of energy, and this applies not only to mechanical or physical energies, but also to vital energies. We know that if we want to do a certain amount of mental work, we have to accumulate enough energy in order to be able to do it, and when the energy is used up, we cannot continue the work. This means that the energies of thought or feeling are also limited. They have their quantities just as do heat or electricity, and also they have their intensities. It is possible to think, just by one idea at a time, with a few degrees of thought energy. If we want to put two or three or four thoughts together, a greater intensity is needed. We know very well that, at some point, we can no longer summon up the required intensity and our thinking loses its power. There is not sufficient "voltage" in any of us to be able to think of seven or eight thoughts at a time. Yet we can believe that someone might be able to do that, if he knows how to produce thought energy of sufficiently high intensity. He would then be able to think far more complicated and much richer thoughts than we are able to. But it will be the same kind of energy all the same. It is not the energy of a higher level of consciousness, nor the energy of unconscious reflexes: it is always the energy of thought, but it may be at a higher voltage or it may be of a lower voltage.

In short, for anything we have to do, energy has to be right in three different ways. It has to be the right **kind**, it has to have the necessary **intensity**, and there must be a sufficient **quantity** of it.

We shall come later to the practical question of producing, storing, and manipulating the energies required for different purposes. Before we come to that, we must have a language in which to speak of these things. We shall construct this language by making a classification of energies, with their respective qualities and properties.

THE PRINCIPAL DIVISIONS

The first division, as far as qualities of energy goes, is into the **mechanical** or physical energies, the **life** energies, and the **cosmic** or universal energies. In each of these main classes, there are many different varieties of energy; but it is possible to say nearly everything that we have to say about energies by dividing each of the three classes into four kinds or qualities. The basis of the division into four is this: we can see for ourselves that there is some kind of gradation or scale of energy. There are energies of a lower quality or energies of a higher quality. It means something to us to say that life energies are on a higher level than mechanical energies, and that cosmic energies are on a higher level than life energies. And within each of these classes there are also different levels. There is something which characterizes the top and the bottom of each class, and one can call these the **plus side** and the **minus side** of each of these energies. For example, with the mechanical energies, the minus side, or character, is that they have no shape, no organization. They are what we can call "**dispersed**," that is, random and chaotic. That is the minus, or negative, aspect of mechanical energy. On the other side, it can be organized, form a particular pattern, and be used in a very special and definite way. Therefore, we can call "**organization**" the positive or plus side of mechanical energy. This distinction leads to a simple method of classification that gives us four kinds for each main class of energy:

TABLE 1
PLUS AND MINUS CHARACTERISTICS

+ +   plus-plus, or dominated by the positive characteristic

+ -   plus-minus, or sharing in both the characteristics with the positive the stronger of the two

- +   minus-plus, or sharing in both with the negative stronger

- -   minus-minus, or dominated by the negative characteristic

This way of distinguishing qualities is useful, but I must make it clear that it is only approximate. There are many intermediate grades and one cannot always be sure that one has assigned a particular energy to the correct division. Then again we seldom meet with energies in a pure state, but rather with blends and this also can make it difficult to know just what we are dealing with. There is also a more radical limitation that comes from the fact that the simple distinction of "higher" and "lower" qualities is only partly valid. The plus-minus and minus-plus qualities are, for many purposes, to be taken on the same level. I cannot go into all these distinctions here and will give the picture in a simplified form.

THE MECHANICAL ENERGIES — DISPERSED ENERGY

We can say that minus-minus mechanical energy is **dispersed energy**, because its chief and only characteristic is that it is dispersed and has no organization. That is the kind of energy that we know as **heat**. Heat is the lowest, least organized, most insensitive of all kinds of energy. It has no place of its own, it has no form of its own, no pattern of its own. Everything contains heat, everything that exists — air, water, our bodies, planets and stars. And heat just flows through everything quite passively. It has a certain character of intensity that we call temperature, and it always flows from where there is more intensity to where there is less intensity. That is to say, it has no direction or organization of its own. That is why I have marked it minus-minus; it has neither any inner organization nor any outer organization. Heat consists in this: that every tiny little particle of matter is in motion — vibrating, moving from one place to another, turning round and round — and in all of these tiny motions, there is a certain amount of energy. But it is quite random, quite chaotic, or what we call **dispersed**. At the same time, it does not mean that this energy is useless, because we know very well that everything requires a certain amount of heat in order to be able to be what it is. You know how dependent our own bodies are upon being at the right temperature. This means that they have to be able to take in the right amount of heat to make up for what they lose. But, although heat is necessary, there is nothing that it is able to do by itself. That is the first and lowest quality of mechanical energy.

DIRECTED ENERGY

The second quality of energy appears wherever there is a direction. For example, if a train is moving along rails, it has energy derived from its motion. That energy has also the direction in which the train is going. Or, if we look at things lying here on the table — glasses, water jugs — they all have a certain amount of energy that comes from the fact that they are in what is called the "gravitational field of the earth." This means that they are being pulled towards the centre of the earth and from that they acquire an energy which has a direction of its own. That is to say, the energy in these objects lying on the table is not only a certain quantity and a certain intensity, but it is also directed. This kind of energy is sometimes called "dynamical," but we shall use the term **directed** energy. The fact that it has a direction is the first step in having some quality of energy which is lacking in heat energy.

You know also how it is with electrical energy: if we electrify certain materials, such as a piece of amber, it will attract light bodies towards it. The same with a magnet which will attract pieces of iron. All round such electrified or magnetized bodies there is energy of attraction. But it is always in a definite direction, so that a body will always move in one direction when it is brought near them. Direction arises from the combination of two different things: one is this action and the other is its own movement. For example, if I were to throw a ball from where I am sitting, it would begin to move in the direction in which I throw it, but little by little the lines of its movement will bend over and it will finally come down on to the earth. It is the same with the way the planets go round the sun. The kind of directed energy that depends upon movement and the attraction of gravitation, electricity and magnetism, is very important. Directed energies already begin to have something more organized about them than the dispersed energy of heat. At the same time they do not hold together in any sort of way. That means that whatever direction they may have, they have no pattern except that they go toward something. We shall call it **directed energy** and put it in Table 1 as minus-plus mechanical energy to show that the dispersed character still predominates over the organized.

COHESIVE ENERGY

The third kind of energy is the one marked plus-minus. These energies are of quite a different kind from either of the first two. They comprise all the energies by which everything is held together. They include what we call "chemical energies." All things we see round us — all solid bodies, the earth and all that is on its surface; all liquids, rivers, and seas — are held together in a particular pattern because there are energies that bind them; and when these energies are studied it turns out that they have another property: that there is always something which is shared in them, and that is why the plus is put on the outside. They are connected together because here always something is shared. And that property of connectedness means that they are able to do all kinds of things that are very necessary. For example, we could not be sitting here if our bodies had not some of this energy of connectedness in them — we could not be sitting on the chairs unless the chairs had some of this energy of connectedness in them. We call this third kind of energy **cohesive energy**. One form of **cohesive energy** is that of chemical bonding. Cohesive energy is the source of the persistence of all kinds of bodies. It is much more highly organized than directed energy.

PLASTIC ENERGY

The fourth kind of mechanical energy, which is marked plus-plus, has a two-fold organization. This enables it to keep a pattern of its own by which it is able to hold together by itself. It is able to move about and yet remain what it is. That is why I shall call this fourth kind **plastic energy**. By "plastic," I mean the property of changing shape without losing coherence. Elasticity, rigidity, and the liquid state of matter are all consequences of the presence of plastic energy. For example, our bodies are pervaded with plastic energy which always adapts itself to the pattern of our bodies and goes about with them. The fourth kind of energy is of that sort. Not only our own bodies have it, but everything else. Sometimes this is called "free," "structural," or "fluid" energy, but I will call it "plastic" energy to remind us that it does not depend upon a fixed shape. I could have called it "organized" except that all energies are more or less organized, so that the differences in quality depend upon the kind of organization. A highly organized energy is a high energy: a disorganized energy is a low one. Plastic energy is the highest kind of energy possible without life.

We can now summarize these results in a diagram:

TABLE 2
THE FOUR KINDS OF MECHANICAL ENERGY

Character	Name of Energy	Examples
+ +	Plastic Energy	Elasticity
+ -	Cohesive Energy	Chemical
- +	Directed Energy	Motion, gravitation and magnetism
- -	Dispersed Energy	Heat

These four energies are present everywhere, though the higher energies are more concentrated in the more highly organized forms of existence.

THE ENERGIES OF LIFE

The simplest property of life is **organization**. Everything that is alive is to some extent organized. Therefore, beyond the highest level of mechanicalness is the lowest or minus property of life; and the highest property of life is **consciousness**, which is plus-plus. So here again, we have the plus-plus, the plus-minus, the minus-plus and the minus-minus, making four levels of life energy.

CONSTRUCTIVE ENERGY

The first and simplest level of life energy is that which gives the power of organization. Life is always organizing the materials it is taking in, producing the different kinds of bodies that are required for plants, animals, and so on. This organizing energy has itself, of course, to be organized. It has not only a pattern of its own, but it has the power to produce patterns in other things. That power is sometimes called "catalytic," which means that it has the power of accelerating or helping a change without being itself changed. Everything that is alive depends upon these organizing powers, and all that we can learn about life shows us more and more how important a part, at the basis of life, is played by all these energies that have organizing power. I shall call these **constructive energies**.

Until recently, constructive energy was unknown to science. When I wrote *The Dramatic Universe*, the only evidence I could give of its existence was in the activity of enzymes and hormones which bring about transformations in the vital fluids — blood and sap — that connect raw materials of the non-living world into the substances required for life. Since *The Dramatic Universe* was published, biological science has made one of the greatest steps forward toward understanding the foundations upon which bodies are built and life processes maintained. This is the discovery of the power of certain nucleic acids (DNA) to promote and regulate the synthesis of the animal life substance, protein. It is now universally expected that this discovery will eventually lead to the artificial production of living forms; but there are no precise ideas as to the nature of the "power" itself, beyond the fact that it is as much structured as causal. It seems to me that I may fairly claim to have predicted this discovery when I wrote, "We may describe the primary life energy as 'constructive' to emphasize the power of breaking down the material of its environment in order to rebuild it into its own tissue." Workers in the field of the nucleic acids agree that an "organized and organizing energy" is at work. Constructive energy stands on the threshold of life. Life does not begin — properly speaking — and really enter, until the positive features connected with consciousness make their appearance.

VITAL ENERGY

The second stage I shall simply call **vital energy**. The vital energy is of quite a different quality from constructive energy, which can also be present in non-living things. Vital energy is experienced by us in what we call vitality — or sometimes simply "energy." It flows in our blood and it flows in our nervous system. It is the vital fire by which everything alive is able to maintain itself on a different level from all that is dead. As soon as this energy loses its organization in any body, that body dies and the vital energy is set free to go and be re-absorbed into other living things. Let me make it clear that the vital energy is a material substance, not an immaterial principle like the *Entelechy* of Driesch or Bergson's *Elan Vital*. Vital energy, like all other forms of energy, has quality, intensity, and quantity, and differs from lower forms only by its incomparably higher degree of organization. Its role can best be seen in the development of organisms after the fertilization of the ovum.

AUTOMATIC ENERGY

The third kind of life energy is associated with the vital functions rather than life itself. I find it very difficult to choose a good word for it, but I think the right word is **automatic energy**. This is the energy of all our automatic functioning. One must not think that mechanical things are automatic. The word "automatic" really means "self-acting." Whereas so-called mechanical automata have to be wound up, an animal is a real automaton, that is to say, something which works by itself with a particular kind of energy that makes it possible. It is already a very highly organized, very sensitive kind of energy. All our automatic associations, all the automatic work of our senses — all automatic seeing, hearing, all our movements that have no intention or choice in them but are simply what are called sometimes reflex movements — all these depend upon automatic energy. As you know, we spend a great deal of our lives with no higher quality of energy working in us than this. Although this kind of energy is plus on the outside, it is minus on the inside. Outwardly, it enables us to behave as we do behave, as if we were free and independent beings. But inside, nothing is there; inwardly we are still machines. That is why this is written plus-minus and why I call it "automatic" energy.

SENSITIVE ENERGY

The plus-plus energy of life begins to be something of our own, inwardly as well as outwardly. I call it **sensitive energy**. When I become sensitive to what is happening to me — as soon as I begin to be aware of my thoughts, of my feelings, of my body, my sensations — this energy is beginning to work in me. Without this fourth, or sensitive, energy, we are nothing but machines. Up to that point there is nothing but mechanicalness, but as soon as sensitive energy enters, the possibility of separating from our own automatism begins. And to have that possibility means really to be alive. Not alive just as a piece of flesh is alive, for which only the second or vital energy is enough, and not to be alive as an animal is alive, for which the third kind of life energy is enough; but alive in the sense of a being who is aware that he exists: not only feels alive but knows what it means: who remembers the past and looks forward into the future. All those things come only through the presence of the fourth or sensitive kind of energy, or what we can call the plus-plus energy of life.

I must draw your attention here to a rather dangerous pitfall on the way to understanding ourselves. This is the tendency to confuse sensitivity and consciousness. We are accustomed to regard as conscious the state in which we are aware of the functional activities of sensation, feeling and thought. Psychologists refer to the "stream of consciousness" wherein the condition is no more than the flow of sensitive energy. Gurdjieff, in his teaching, constantly refers to the error of confusing this with true consciousness, which man scarcely ever notices. Sensitivity is no more than the "fullness of life," whereas consciousness is contact with the central fact of our own individuality.

TABLE 3
THE FOUR KINDS OF LIFE ENERGY

Character	Name of Energy	Examples
+ +	Sensitive energy	Awareness of experience. Separation from automatism
+ -	Automatic energy	Automatic sensations and movements
- +	Vital energy	Nervous energy, "vitality"
- -	Constructive energy	DNA, enzymes and hormones

UNIVERSAL ENERGIES

Now we come to the cosmic or universal energies. The lowest characteristic of the universal energies, or their minus-minus, is **consciousness**, which is the highest point of life energy; and the highest energy is that which has originated and now sustains the whole of existence as a self-consistent totality. Such an energy must have its roots beyond existence itself, and we shall therefore call it **Transcendent**. In the very notion of universal energies there is something that goes beyond experience, and we can take it that all the cosmic energies have different degrees of transcendence, but only at the limit of the plus-plus cosmic energy is existence itself left behind. Another name for transcendent energy is "Divine Creative Power," but this seems to imply some kind of theistic belief which does not enter the discussion of energies as such. It is enough that we associate the dynamism of "All Existence" with the highest possible kind of energy.

CONSCIOUS ENERGY

It may seem strange to you that **consciousness** should be taken as a cosmic rather than a life energy, and you may ask, "How is it that we human beings can have consciousness? How is it that this cosmic energy can belong to us?" But it is really not true that we have consciousness — we can participate *in* consciousness, but consciousness is never *our* consciousness, and anyone who has come to some understanding and some real experience of this will know very well what I say, that although our sensitivity — our power, let us say, of observing and separating ourselves — can be our own, consciousness is never our own. Consciousness is always something greater than we are, and we really do not understand how much greater because we do not see that consciousness is everywhere and we can only have a part in it. At the same time, because it is the minus-minus energy among the four cosmic energies, we are able to reach it, and the experience of it does enter into us; but it always has this certain quality of being something greater than we are at that moment that it comes to us.

The second of the cosmic energies is beyond consciousness and has a hidden quality that connects it with the creative activity by which the Universe is incessantly renewed. For this reason, I have called it the **creative energy**. Notwithstanding its transcendental character, it plays an essential part in our lives as the source of the power by which life is generated. It acts through the sex function of man, though few people realize that the power of sex is beyond sensitivity and even consciousness. It might be supposed that this energy is not only conscious but familiar to us all; but we confuse the sensitive energy associated with the experience of sex with the creative energy which transmits the **power** of sex.

The all-important creative energy is the source of all human creativity of which procreation is no more than the vital manifestation. All that man creates in practical affairs, in science and in art, depends upon the working of the creative energy. In a higher sense, the creative energy is the Great Force of Life by which all existence is pervaded. This is the energy that acts upon us in what Gurdjieff calls the *second conscious shock,* by which our nature is purified. It is the highest energy that plays a direct part in human experience.

We know almost nothing about the two highest kinds of cosmic energy, and yet their action pervades everything. But you must understand that we can never have more than an indirect realization of their presence, because there is nothing in man that can respond directly to these energies, except perhaps for a moment, like seeing a flash of lightning.

The third energy is called the **unitive energy**, for the reason that it is by this energy that everything, everywhere in the whole universe, is being constantly integrated and made whole. It is marked plus-minus because it is the inner energy that acts upon every consciousness. This means that in the deepest part of every living creature there is a realization that there is a force that is directed towards our true welfare. At the same time, you must remember that this higher energy is beyond the range of the powers of man. The energy of the Unitive Power can reach us only indirectly. It has to be transmitted through something else, about which we will speak later.

The fourth and highest energy is still more incomprehensible for us, because we can neither know its action nor know how it is organized in the universe. It concerns us only on the grounds that a significant whole must contain at least all that is significant in its parts. If dynamism is important on any level, then it must be most important on the highest level. The term "transcendent energy" expresses the belief that if there is movement there is a Prime Mover, if there is Creation then there is a Creative Source. We can put the four cosmic energies into a table:

TABLE 4
THE FOUR COSMIC ENERGIES

Character	Name of Energy	Operation
+ +	Transcendent	The Supreme Will
+ -	Unitive	Universal Love
- +	Creative	Generation and Creation
- -	Conscious	Man's "I", Will

THE TABLE OF TWELVE ENERGIES

We can now make a complete table of all the kinds of energy in the universe:

TABLE 5
THE TWELVE ENERGIES

Cosmic Energies

Transcendent Energy	E1
Unitive Energy	E2
Creative Energy	E3
Conscious Energy	E4

Life Energies

Sensitive Energy	E5
Automatic Energy	E6
Vital Energy	E7
Constructive Energy	E8

Mechanical Energies

Plastic Energy	E9
Cohesive Energy	E10
Directed Energy	E11
Dispersed Energy	E12

These twelve energies and the qualities that characterize them give rise to all the infinitely complex activity of all that exists. This, of course, includes us men and all the qualities of energies that can enter into our human experience. Each one of the twelve is important for us, whether it reaches beyond us, like the highest energies, or whether it is simply one of the mechanical energies upon which the work of our bodies depends.

Later, we shall see how they can be transformed, and what is meant by the transformation of energy from one quality into another. The whole secret of our existence lies in the fact that energy of one quality can be transformed into energy of another quality.

⊹

QUESTIONS

Q. Do I understand that the highest positive consciousness that we can have is a negative consciousness on a higher level?
J.G.B. Yes, that is nearly right. What is positive in one direction is negative in the other direction. The highest sensitivity that belongs to life alone is really a denying energy in relation to the cosmic energies. But we do not know consciousness "from above."

Q. It acts as a denying force to the higher?
J.G.B. Yes. The diagram suggests that there is in man something more than just life. Man is something more than a living being; he has something in him which participates in energies that are beyond life — that is, in the cosmic energies.

Q. What is the relation between force and energy?
J.G.B. Force comes from the action between an energy of one intensity and an energy of another intensity. Force comes from the separation of one intensity from another.

Q. Can you explain plastic energy? I am not quite clear from the example you gave.
J.G.B. No one word will convey all that is wanted. I might also have said adaptive energy. By plasticity, solid things are changing the whole time, and yet in some way, although they change they still remain themselves. For instance, if I take water in a jug and pour it into a glass, its shape will change, but it will still be water. It is able to do that because it has something in it which enables it

to be itself and yet go through a limited amount of change; that we may call adaptiveness. We can recognize plastic energy in what we call deformation. It is the highest property of ordinary things that are not alive: they have a certain power of adaptation, a certain flexibility or plasticity. In order to have that, they have to have something more than just the connectedness that is sufficient, let us say, to make a crystal keep its shape.

Q. Has a human being a certain overall quantity of energy to be distributed between levels?
J.G.B. No. Each level has its separate account, as it were, although there can be transformation of one kind into another. For example, we have a certain amount of heat in our bodies. That heat is being lost all the time; it has to be renewed in some way or another. A small proportion of the heat energy in our bodies is converted into directed energy; for example, in maintaining the flow of our blood. But something more than heat alone is required to maintain the circulation of the blood and what is called the general "tone" of the nervous system. The mechanical activity of our bodies requires the second kind of mechanical energy. We need a certain quantity at a time of directed energy in our bodies, quite apart from the amount of heat energy we need. We were talking about plastic energy just now. We need a certain quantity of this also: the adaptibility and flexibility of our bodies depend upon the quantity of plastic energy available. This energy comes from connected energy, but unless there are means of converting one into another, a quantity of one kind of energy will not make up for a deficiency of another kind.

Q. May I ask you about the "voltage" of the highest cosmic energy? If it should contact a person by accident, what happens? Or doesn't it touch us at all?
J.G.B. Yes, it can — but it is rather like being struck by lightning! You understand, electricity is all very fine in its way, but lightning is a bit much to cope with. It is like that; this is very, very high

voltage, and that is why I say that if by chance it touches someone, they have a very big shock from it, and they need a lightning conductor of some sort.

Q. That is exactly what I was going to ask you — what is this lightning conductor?

J.G.B. It appears that an energy of a lower quality can act as a carrier of an energy of a higher quality. But it cannot do so unless things have been prepared in the right way. The simile of a lightning conductor is a very good one: you can have a lightning conductor that consists, let us say, of a band of copper. But that band of copper has to be arranged so that it goes up to the top of the house and it has to be arranged so that the other end goes into the earth. When it does that, then it is able to carry off enough of the electricity not to smash everything. In the same way, there is in each one of us a special kind of lightning conductor for carrying off these high energies — so that, although they are present all the time, they are all the time bypassing us. You do not have to make a new lightning conductor, but you have to find out where something has become disconnected in the lightning conductor. If we were not made with lightning conductors, all of us would be destroyed by these high energies.

Q. Are buffers lightning conductors?

J.G.B. Yes, of a kind, but they are lightning conductors against much, much milder energies than the creative energy we have been talking about, and they are made for our convenience, because people do not want to have the kind of shocks that are really necessary for them.

Q. Could you say something about the energy by which living beings grow?

J.G.B. All four kinds of life energy enter into everything that is alive. The highest, sensitive energy, carries the pattern of the particular organism — that is what we call its essence. Through it, the organism is related to the pattern of its own species. It relates every dog to the pattern of Dog, every oak to the pattern of Oak, and so on. And each essence as soon as it is formed, at the moment of conception, or fertilization of the ovum, is formed as a pattern of sensitive energy. The sensitive energy carries that pattern all through the rest of its life. The life energy that I called "automatic" maintains all the adjustments between this essence pattern and the various processes of life. It forms the regulative mechanism of life itself. It operates throughout the development of the embryo, up to and beyond the moment of birth, right to the end of life. Every living organism depends upon incessant adjustment or regulation which takes place through the automatic energy. The vital energy is associated with the cellular foundation of life in all the various tissues. The lowest of the four life energies is that which builds up the materials required by every kind of organism: they include carbohydrates, fats, and proteins, sometimes of immense complexity and always very exactly adapted for particular requirements. The constructive energy maintains the "bio-synthetic" activity of substances like DNA.

Q. Where does the energy of atomic power come in? Is it a very low energy, or a very high fine energy?
J.G.B. It is the connected energy. If that energy is set free, it is very much more powerful than the lower mechanical energies.

Q. Can you say why you use the word "sensitive"? It is rather an unusual use of the word, I think.
J.G.B. I could have used a term like "psychic energy," but this has misleading associations. Sensitivity is a property shared by all the higher forms of life and, I personally believe, by all life even down to the level of viruses and protoplasm itself. When it is sufficiently concentrated, that is when its intensity reaches a certain degree, it produces awareness. This is very easy to recognize with the sensation of heat and cold. We are usually unaware of the state of our skin; but when the temperature rises or falls beyond well-defined

limits, we say that we "feel" hot or cold. If it goes further still, we "feel" pain. Sensation and pain are different degrees of sensitivity.

You must also understand that sensitivity can be organized. Let us go back to the question put to me just now: what is it that directs the development of an organism and what is it that, when an organism is developed, maintains the organism more or less true to its own pattern? Sensitive energy does that, because it is able to respond both to energies finer than itself and also to energies lower than itself. That is what I mean by "sensitivity."

We can confirm this in our own experience. My eyes are looking all the time and I am seeing the door opposite, but I do not **notice** it. When I notice it, there is a complete change, and I realize that a new quality of energy is present in me that was not there before. What makes it possible for me to notice is that the energy of sensitivity has been added to the bare energy of auto-matism. I may be speaking, but it is my automatism that speaks, and I may not be sensitive to what I am saying. Then something changes in me and some of this energy of sensitivity is added; I then become **aware** of what I am saying. When that energy is used up or goes off into something else, I may still go on speaking, but it is only my automatism speaking. I no longer hear what I am saying. This does not mean that sensitivity totally disappears — if it were so we should die — but that its intensity has fallen below the threshold of awareness.

Q. Why did you say that the four highest energies are higher than life? Are they not higher aspects of living?
J.G.B. By "life" I mean what we usually call life; that is, the terrestrial existence of plants, animals, and men. But there is something beyond that. To be conscious is not simply another aspect of life, it is something that is altogether more than life.

Q. But it is contained in life?
J.G.B. On the contrary; life is contained in it. Life cannot possibly contain consciousness, it is much too small a vessel to contain

consciousness. One can be dead and still be conscious. But one cannot be dead and still be sensitive. If you can understand this, you will understand a great deal about what happens to us when we die.

✠

LECTURE II

The Transformations
of Energy

OUR NEXT TASK IS TO STUDY the **transformations of energy**. By this we mean the passage from one quality to another quality. The main transformations are the conversions of any one of the twelve qualities into a higher or lower quality. The upgrading of energy is called **anabolic transformation** and the downgrading of energy is called **katabolic transformation**.

Not all energy changes are, in the true sense, "transformations." Changes of intensity without change of quality are occurring all the time. For example, a hot body exposed to cold air soon cools down. The intensity of thermal energy diminishes; but whether hot or cold, heat remains heat and does not change into another quality. The transformations of energy differ in several ways from changes of intensity. The most important difference is that they never occur independently. For one quality of energy to be transformed into another, it is always necessary that a third kind should act on it. One of the simplest examples is the conversion of the energy of motion into heat. This seems to occur spontaneously whenever a moving body is brought to rest — as, for example, when we put on the brakes of a car. But if there were no brakes, the car would not slow down and there would be no heat. So the **connected** energy of the material from which the brakes are

25

made must be present so that the **directed** energy of motion should
have the means of producing heat. Such an arrangement is katabolic, for heat energy is a lower quality than the energy of
motion. For anabolic transformations, it is necessary to have
special conditions that I shall refer to as the **apparatus**. We can
define "apparatus" as the means whereby anabolic conversions of
energy are made possible.

Before we begin to study examples, I want you to remember
that each of these twelve main qualities or categories of energy has
its own subdivisions, so that when we meet with a particular
energy, it is usually a mixture of several different shades of quality.
This makes the study of the transformations of energy very complicated; so, in order to be able to think about it profitably, we have
to simplify and treat mixtures as if they were pure energies, and
also disregard many subordinate transformations leading in different directions. But you must not forget that this simplification is
artificial, and that, in the real world, the transformation of energy
is very complex.

In this lecture, I shall examine five or six examples of transformation. In one or two cases, I will show you how the transformation of one quality of energy into another quality may bring
about a whole lot of other secondary transformations. The transformation of energies was called, in former times, "the separation
of the fine from the coarse." We are inclined to think of that as
improving or raising the quality of energy, but we must not forget
that as one part of the energy is raised in quality, it inevitably
happens that another part is debased. If some goes up, some must
also go down.

Another thing I want to say before I begin to discuss examples
is that we must not forget that energy is not what we see. **Energies**
are hidden away, they are not in the same dimension as the **things**
which we touch, handle, see, measure. There can, for example,
be two substances that may look very much alike, and even when
tested physically or chemically seem to behave in much the same
way; but one may contain energy of a very different quality from

the other. In our bodies, there are a relatively small number — by that I mean something like forty or fifty perhaps — highly specialized chemical substances, each of which carries a particular kind of energy essential for maintaining the delicate equilibria of our organic and psychic existence. If one knew about them only chemically, one would not suspect that they had these extraordinary properties. Each one is able to carry or to support a particular quality of energy because it is made according to a very precise pattern. It is not the substance itself which is the energy and it is not the substance itself which is important for our study. For example, there is one particular substance, called adenosine triphosphate, that exists in the bodies of all animals, and has the property of being able to store and make immediately available at any moment a very large quantity of a particular energy that can help in building up the tissues of the body and even higher substances. I think it is safe to say that no chemist, given a sample of adenosine triphosphate to examine without knowing its biological significance, would suspect that it has this extraordinary property of being able to act as a medium for transforming the energies necessary for life. There are in our blood and in all our tissues many such substances that help in the conversion and transformation of energy. They include the substances which go by the name of "enzymes." These are very complex, and millions upon millions of quite different kinds of such substances could exist; but just a very few of them are present in our bodies to carry the particular energies required for the life of our organism. If you study metabolism — that is, the transformation of energies in animals and plants — you will find references to particular chemical substances that have certain properties in the working of the organism. But when you read carefully, you cannot help seeing that these special substances must have more in them than a particular chemical composition. Every year this becomes clearer. When I first gave a lecture in 1930 on the subject of energies, I spoke then about this property of certain chemical substances that enables them to act as the carriers of different qualities of energy.

In the short time of twenty-six years since I gave that lecture, such progress has been made in the branch of science called "bio-chemistry," that what then seemed very strange has now become a commonplace of science. Two or three chemists who came to that lecture were so shocked by what I said that they went away and never came again. But biochemists today would not be at all astonished at what I have just been saying — though you will realize that the idea of a whole scale of energies ranging from heat right up to the Power that Maintains the Unity of Existence must necessarily go beyond any and even all branches of natural science.

Now let us examine a few examples of the transformation of energy. I will discuss first the transformation of Energy 12 into Energy 11; that is, transformation of the dispersed energy, which is the lowest, (heat) into directed energy, which means energy which can be used for doing mechanical work — whether it is the work of the muscles in our bodies or the work of engines. Heat alone will not do any work. In order to get work from heat, it is necessary to have two different sources, one hot and one cold. Then the flow of heat from hot to cold acquires a direction, but to turn this flow into mechanical energy a particular kind of appa-ratus is used, called a heat engine. But in that case, the heat has already been divided into hot and cold.

Supposing that there were a certain quantity of heat which was not divided at all, without any difference of intensity — could any work be got out of that? With an ordinary heat engine, no work could be got, because heat can only flow from what is hot to what is cold. But what is heat? We spoke about it in the previous lecture. It is all the energy that is stored up in countless millions of millions of particles — in air, solid bodies, liquids — moving, vibrating, and rotating at random. The faster they move, the more energy they carry and the "hotter" they are. Because they are always colliding with one another and with the walls of their container, the particles of gas quickly share any surplus energy and reach what is called "equipartition," in which no further flow of heat occurs and therefore no transformation is possible. However, it was shown nearly a hundred years ago that if one had a quantity of gas in this state of equipartition, it would be still possible, by the use of intelligence, to get work out of its heat, even though the intelligence had no direct power of doing physical work. That is very interesting, because it was perhaps the first time in the history of modern science that one of the fundamental principles of the transformation of energies, as we understand it in our system, was formulated. The idea was put forward by the great Scottish mathematician Clarke Maxwell. He said, "Suppose we had a box and put a wall down the middle with a door so light and free from friction as not to require any work to open and shut it, and small enough to catch individual molecules of the gas.

FIG. 1
HEAT ENGINE

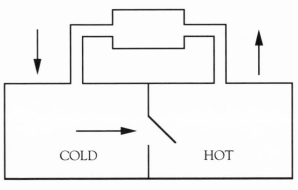

THE SORTING DEMON

"Now suppose there is a being — a 'sorting demon' — who does not have to do any work but is able with automatic energy, E6, to open the door or to close it according to whether he sees fast or slow moving particles going past him. Sometimes they move in all directions, sometimes one will come to this door. If the sorting demon opens the door to let the fast ones go to the right, and if he opens it to the left for the slow ones, the right side will get hot and the left side will get cold."

FIG. 2
THE POWER OF THOUGHT

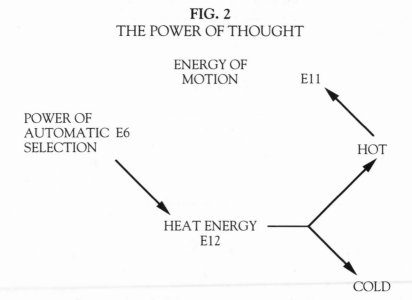

When the gas on the right side has grown very hot and that on the left very cold, it is possible to open the pipe at the top of the box and pass it through a heat engine to get mechanical energy. In this way it would be possible, by the action of E6 on E12, to get a supply of E11. At the same time, E12 will have fallen to a lower intensity than before. This is a simple demonstration that there can be a transformation of energy in a suitable kind of apparatus by the action of an energy of a higher order. The action can be shown by means of a simple diagram (see Figure 2):

Now we shall go forward a step to another kind of transformation. The energies that we call E11 are carried by simple substances like air, water, and sunlight. In a very special kind of apparatus that exists in the green leaves of plants there is a means by which a special substance, having the density of E8, acts on the mixture of air, water, and sunlight and produces from it E10 — in

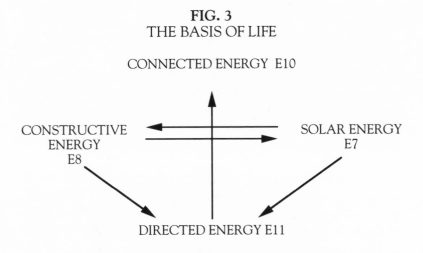

FIG. 3
THE BASIS OF LIFE

CONNECTED ENERGY E10

CONSTRUCTIVE
ENERGY
E8

SOLAR ENERGY
E7

DIRECTED ENERGY E11

this case various carbohydrates, which are mainly cellulose. In the process, E12 energy is absorbed in the form of heat. At the same time there is produced some E11 in the form of oxygen and water. The process is called "photosynthesis."

The transformations of photosynthesis are represented by the diagram of Figure 3.

Photosynthesis is perhaps the most important energy transformation that takes place on the surface of our earth. All life depends upon it: it is possible only in the presence of certain particular substances that belong to that group of energies called E8, energies of a constructive power, the power to build up. Last week I spoke about catalysts, or substances that are able to promote or accelerate changes without themselves being involved. The particular E8 which is mainly responsible for photosynthesis is the green pigment chlorophyll, present in all green vegetation on the earth and in the sea. An extraordinarily large proportion of all the sunlight that falls on the earth is absorbed by green vegetation — four-fifths of it in the sea and one-fifth on the land — and it passes through that transformation with water and the carbon dioxide in the air.

Something like a hundred thousand million tons of carbohydrates are made every year on the surface of the earth by this one process of transformation. This is the first example we know of a **cosmic apparatus** for the transformation of energy. The chlorophyll in the cells of all green vegetation is combined with substances of the E9 and E10 qualities into a particular arrangement. It is connected with fats and proteins and cellulose tissues, all of which build up a particular kind of apparatus that enables this really prodigious transformation of energy to be accomplished. Photosynthesis transforms energy of a quality that could not be formed independently. It is this alone that makes life possible on the planet. Life needs connected energy (E10) in a particularly concentrated form. The energy made by this transformation is the foundation of the food of all plants, of all animals, and of all men. Very small quantities of food are made by bacteria and by other processes than this, but the transformation shown in Figure 3 is the main cosmic process for the preparation of food for all living things on the earth. And no one has yet found a way of producing this process without the help of some higher energy of the quality I call E8. The process can go in the katabolic direction — E10 can degenerate into E11 — automatically, without any help of higher energies. That is the destructive process by which we burn any vegetable or animal matter in air or oxygen. That is the reversing of the arrow, by which such matter turns back into air, water, and light. But to unburn, to produce the anabolic concentration of energy that is required for life, is possible only if there is some higher energy to act as the third force in the process.

The third example I shall take, is the process by which we digest food. Food belongs to the E10 energies. You must not forget what I said: that it is not the particular chemical substance — potato, meat, and so on — that constitutes food, but the presence in it of energy of suitable quality that has the power of connecting things and building a body. When food (E10) is taken into the body, there acts on it substances of E8 quality. These are the ferments or digestive juices that meet the food from the moment it enters the mouth until it has been liquified and turned into what is called chyle — that is, E9 — and is able to pass through the membranes of the intestinal tract and enter into the body. When this is done, E10 is split up and the resulting energies go in several different directions. Part is just stored up in the body in the form of substances that simply contain this energy in easily disposable form, E10 substances such as glycogen and fats. Part of this energy goes downwards to become E11 — that is, the directed energy that is used for the working of our muscles. This is the energy that enables our bodies to work as machines, as heat engines. It is muscular energy. And this again, as it is used, goes on down into E12 and simply becomes the heat needed to keep our bodies warm. In ordinary biological language all that is called "katabolism," or the downward movement of energy; it is what I have called katabolic transformation. From this process, energies of lower qualities are produced that enable the body to work. But at the same time a proportion of these energies is built up into the mobile

FIG. 4
THE PRIMARY METABOLISM OF MEN AND ANIMALS

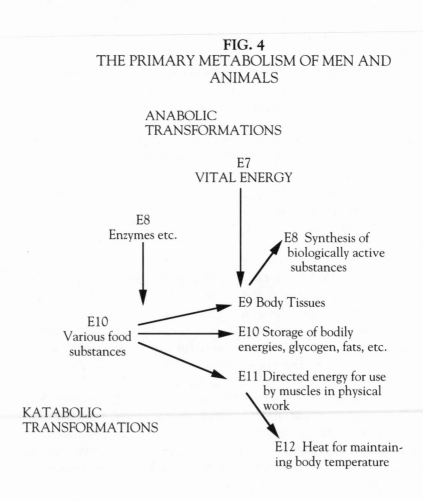

ANABOLIC
TRANSFORMATIONS

E7
VITAL ENERGY

E8
Enzymes etc.

E8 Synthesis of
biologically active
substances

E9 Body Tissues

E10
Various food
substances

E10 Storage of bodily
energies, glycogen, fats, etc.

E11 Directed energy for use
by muscles in physical
work

KATABOLIC
TRANSFORMATIONS

E12 Heat for maintain-
ing body temperature

energies, E9, the energies that give our bodies their mobility, their elasticity. They enter into the tissues of the body. One part of the E9 goes into building up the tissues of the body. During childhood a large proportion of the E9 energy has to go to this, as the body is growing, but in later life also there is a constant need of the body for E9 to ensure the renewal and repair of its tissues. Still another part, this time under the influence of the vital energy E7 in the organism, is turned into substances of quality E8. This produces the biologically active substances that regulate the life of the body. We can now put this in the form of a diagram (see Figure 4):

This diagram will help you to see something of the complexity of energy transformations. Whenever energy of a higher quality is produced, energy of a lower quality has always to be produced with it. The diagram summarizes all that is ordinarily known about the metabolism of food in the animal body. Although it looks complicated, if you were to read a textbook on metabolism you would see what a wonderful simplification is achieved when one studies metabolism in terms of energies, instead of chemical substances. I have marked the lower part of the diagram as katabolic and the upper as anabolic, the meaning of which is particularly easy to see here.

The animal organism, which includes our human organism too, is a special cosmic apparatus for the transformation of energy. You will note that it transforms energy of a higher quality than those which are transformed by photosynthesis. The plant begins with E11 and builds it up to E10 and also into higher energies such as those in proteins. You must realize that we depend on plants for our supply of certain substances of quality E9, as we are not able to make them in our own organism out of simple substances of quality E11. If I had made the complete diagram of the plant metabolism it also would have shown a transformation into five different qualities of energies. In *All and Everything*, there are many references to "cosmic apparatuses" for the transformation of energy, and I want you to see now what is meant by a cosmic apparatus. It is a particular construction in which energies can be brought

together so that there can be a transformation to produce both
higher and lower energies. From the point of view of our study —
that is, of what we call **Work** for the harmonious development of
man — it is of course the anabolic transformation of energies that
is of main interest to us. But we must not forget that there is always
a price to be paid. All the anabolic, all the upward, transformations of energy are always made at a price of a certain proportion of
the energy going by way of katabolism to a lower level.

Let us take the transformation of energy one more stage. I
will first show you the corresponding diagram (see Figure 5).

Here we start from E8. The apparatus for the transformation
of E8 is the blood. There are active substances carrying energies in
the blood that can be transformed into still higher energies; but
now we are beginning to pass from the passive energies to energies
that have the property of awareness in them, and such energies can
be produced only at a cost. This means that the transition at this
point requires special conditions in the apparatus. The transformation of the active substances which have reached the threshold
of life as enzymes and hormones can pass to a higher level only
with a special process called "blending."

It is possible to express this in terms of the law of seven-
foldness or octaves, and to say that here at this point there is an
interval in the octave — or the place where the octave stops and
cannot go forward independently. An outside shock is needed.
The transformation of E8 in the blood is possible only when there
is a blending of active substances in the blood with active substances in air, both having the quality of E8. Such energies have in
themselves a building up or anabolic power. But for that anabolic
power itself to be transformed into something higher, it is necessary here to have an action of E6 upon it. This is the action of the
automatic regulative mechanism of the body, which has to be
brought to bear so that E8 can be transformed into E7 which
supplies the body with vital energy. The vitality of the body comes
from the transformation of the active substances in the blood and
the active substances in the air through the help of the energy of

FIG. 5
TRANSFORMATIONS IN THE BLOOD

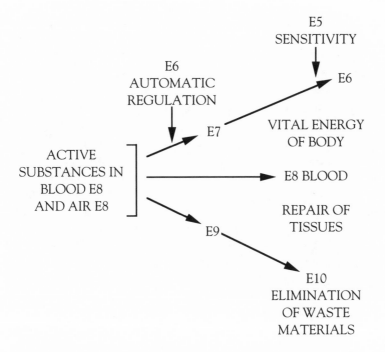

the regulative mechanism of the body. Some of these E8 sub-stances remain as they are, vivify the arterial blood, and endow it with power over the body. Another part of the E8 goes down into E9. This is exactly what is needed for repairing the tissues that are constantly being used up in the activity of the body. Part is katabolised to E10 and goes into the discarded materials that are excreted from the body. These E10 energies enter again into the cycle of transformations of plant life. This is very important for the economy of organic life, but we are mainly concerned with the upward, anabolic movement. The vital energy, E7, under the action this time of sensitive energy, E5, is transformed into E6 — that is, automatic energy. This is done through the sensitivity of our organism to all the processes that are going on in it. This can be called "organic self-experiencing." What is called the "tone" of our nervous system and the state of activity of our blood is maintained by this E6. You will note that this diagram has gone beyond the primary metabolism by which the body as a body is kept going and has entered the vital transformations. Through the mechanism shown in this diagram, our bodies become something more than mere **chemical** apparatuses. They become **vital** apparatuses for the transformation of the energies of life itself.

I will pass over the next step and begin now with E6, which is **automatic energy.** We know about it chiefly in all the automatic working of our functions: our automatic thinking, our reflex movements, and the hole instinctive automatism by which our body is regulated. It includes also all the automatic entry of sense impressions — of sight and of hearing and touch. These are all different varieties of that quality of energy called E6. E6 is the third kind of food for man.

The ordinary working of the human and animal organism is very simple in this case. These energies simply enter the body as E6 and produce all reflex and associative activities. This means that there is no ready-made apparatus for transformation of the E6 that comes to man through his senses. E6 does not have to be transformed for the ordinary purposes of life. It is able to do the work that is necessary for the body while remaining as E6 — that is, by supplying the need for the automatic energy by which the bodily functions are regulated. But of course it is absolutely essential that we should take in this energy the whole time, because otherwise there would be nothing to replenish the automatic energy of the body, which is used up much faster than it can be produced from other sources. All the time the energy of E6 is being fed into our bodies through the nerve endings in the skin, through the special senses of seeing, hearing, taste, and so on. At the same time, the transformation of E6 into higher qualities is also possible, because with the E6 — that is, with the impressions that we receive through our senses — there are also energies of a higher kind. But here it is necessary to understand that the transformation can only take place if there is present some of the higher energy of consciousness — that is, E4 — in order to transform E6 into E5.

FIG. 6
SELF-REMEMBERING

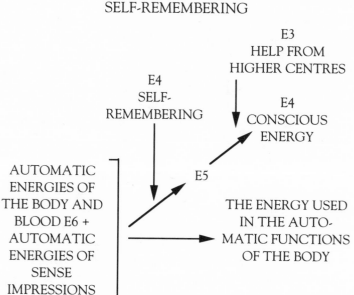

E5 is the energy of sensitivity, and in order to transform automatic energy into sensitivity we need some energy of consciousness. That is why this is called the diagram of **Self-remembering**. It shows that when some energy of consciousness is brought into contact with the energy of impressions, we make in ourselves an apparatus for the transformation of E6 that very greatly increases the supply of sensitive energy, E5. That which comes from the transformation of the other foods is quite insufficient for some of the purposes we shall be talking about later. You must remember, in comparing this diagram with the other ones, that the first two stages of metabolism or transformation of energy are maintained by cosmic apparatuses which form part of the organism, not only of man but of all animals. All warm-blooded animals like man have the metabolic apparatus developed as it is in us. But now we are speaking about an apparatus which is characteristically human and not to be found in animals. You must also understand that it is not to be found in man either, unless he knows how to produce it in himself, or unless something happens to him that "injects" the energy of consciousness into him, involuntarily. There are the various emotional shocks that come to us in life, without which this transformation of E5 into E6 would not take place in us at all. And because it is necessary for the purposes of life that there should be a small, but not negligible, quantity of energy of sensitivity and also of the next higher energy E4 in man, there is provided something that should rather be called a "cosmic contrivance" than a "cosmic apparatus." It is not part of the ordinary construction of a being like man that he should be dependent upon unexpected, involuntary shocks to have moments of consciousness, and that is why I call it a "contrivance."

In order to transform the energy of sensitivity into consciousness, there must be a certain action of the creative energy E3. This is a universal, cosmic energy that is always present and therefore a certain transformation of E5 does occur. Consequently, the result of an involuntary emotional shock is to produce some energy of both sensitivity E5 and consciousness E4.

The diagram here represents two different things. It first represents the occasional involuntary awakening of consciousness in man as a result of some external shock, painful or joyful, a shock which is more intense than any of his ordinary experiencing. Producing E4 and E5 by this means was given a very good description by Ouspensky — he called it "living on pennies you pick up in the street," which only gives you a very low standard of living.

The second significance of the diagram is that it represents voluntary self-remembering. Only by self-remembering can we get sufficient output to give us the energy needed for purposes other than just the automatic functioning of our bodies. Man has to learn how to "remember himself," whether it is called by that name or by any other name; he has to bring himself voluntarily under a certain kind of experience that makes him aware of the influences acting on him.

The highest energy produced from E6 is the E4 shown at the top right hand corner of Figure 6. This is produced by a process of which we are usually not conscious at all. It is the action of the Higher Centres that transmit the universal creative energy E3. We have, at present, no material for studying this "higher anabolism" of impressions, but it is needed for completeness as it shows how the organism is supplied with the E4 needed for life.

Now we come to the last of the examples I will give of transformations of energy. This time it is the transformation of E4; that is, consciousness itself. As I have just been saying, there is always produced in man from time to time a certain quantity of conscious energy of E4 as a result of various sharp intense experiences; but for the full perfecting of man, it is essential that he should have something in him that is able to respond to the higher energies, and especially E2. That means that if there is nothing ever produced in him higher than E4 he can never become a free individual, what is called a **being in his own right**. Therefore the anabolic transformation of E4, the energy of consciousness, must be the aim of every religion, of every teaching that is concerned with the possibility of man's reaching the higher worlds of universal consciousness. For this, according to the same relationship, it is necessary to have some energy of E2; that is, energy of cosmic love, which is, of course, not what we usually understand by "love." That E2 energy is always present everywhere and in everything. Therefore it does not need to be brought. It is there, but the ordinary man is not open to it. The energy of consciousness always produces a feeling in him of "I" and the possibility of the transformation of this energy is something really that man is most afraid of, because he feels that if this transformation does take place in him, he will lose his own "I." If he is able to open himself to the action of Cosmic Love, this produces some of the energy of the third kind — the energy of the creative power, which is the real "I" in man. This points to a very strange situation which always exists in people; that is, that the energy which gives us the illusory feeling of "I" is the energy which has to be transformed in order to produce in us the real and permanent I. From the point of view of our ordinary energies, E3 is outside the range of consciousness, and therefore appears like unconsciousness. It is only E3 that gives a being freedom. No one has the possibility of doing, unless he has sufficient E3 energy in him. By the help of E3 a man can be free from his own mechanism. But in order to have E3 it is necessary that the energy of consciousness should be transformed and there is no ready-made apparatus for doing this.

The situation is shown in the last diagram (see Figure 7).

This diagram is sometimes called the "triad of help." It has also been called the symbol of the transformation of the emotional life of man. The best name is the transformation of consciousness, because it is through this energy that the possibility comes for man to rise above human levels. It is not by man's own power but by his being able to open or submit himself to the action of the higher E2 energy that this final transformation takes place.

I have used these six examples to illustrate transformations of energy, but I especially want you to grasp the principles which are involved in this. First, **energy is an invisible power**. It is not this or that chemical substance or this or that material — it is a particular

FIG. 7
THE TRANSMUTATION OF CONSCIOUSNESS

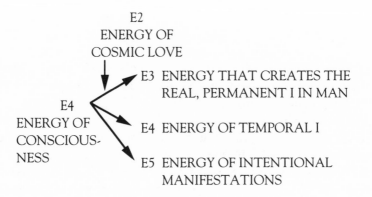

E2
ENERGY OF
COSMIC LOVE

E3 ENERGY THAT CREATES THE
REAL, PERMANENT I IN MAN

E4
ENERGY OF
CONSCIOUS-
NESS

E4 ENERGY OF TEMPORAL I

E5 ENERGY OF INTENTIONAL
MANIFESTATIONS

quality. Second, the transformation of energy from one quality into another always depends upon the **mutual action of two or more energies**. Third, for this mutual action, there has always to be a **special apparatus**, something which holds them together while this action is taking place. We have spoken today of the photosynthesis in green vegetation. This is a great cosmic apparatus on an incomparably greater scale than individual human life. Others, like the first one of the transformation of heat, are the kind of apparatus that the intelligence of man is able to devise. There are other apparatuses that are made naturally as part of the whole cosmic economy. The apparatuses for the transformation of energy in the bodies of animals and men are examples of those. There are again other apparatuses that are only present in us as possibilities. Those are especially the apparatuses for the transformations of higher energies that are formed only through the conscious intention of the being in whom they are present.

⊹

QUESTIONS

Q. When you spoke about the first example, you brought in E6 for the transformation between E12 and E11 — is it not a very high energy for such a purpose?
J.G.B. Yes, that is right, I did. The reason is that the sorting demon apparatus is not cosmic. Only cosmic apparatuses work with full efficiency. This means that they work where energies that are separated by only two gradations can act in order to produce the middle one. But the kind of apparatuses that we men can make are never as efficient as that. They are always much more wasteful in the qualities of energy they use. That is the difference.

Q. Do energies E1, E2, and E3 exist in time?
J.G.B. It is better to say that they are not subject to time conditioning in the same way as the life energies are. There is not a kind of vessel called "time" that things either are "in" or "not in." Rather than speak of "existing in time" it is better to ask whether they are "subject to time" or not. I would reply that they are not subject to the laws of time in the same way as the lower energies are. This applies also to the energy of consciousness. This is something you can verify for yourself. When you learn to distinguish the energy of consciousness from that of sensitivity, you will discover that consciousness does not "move" in the way that sensitivity moves. We experience its presence as the "still and silent place in the centre." Also, we find that consciousness is connected with itself in a way that is quite absent from sensitivity or automatism. We cannot study creative energy in the same way;

but whenever it influences our lives — as it frequently does — we become aware of it as a **result**, never as a **process**. In other words, it gives no indication of being subject to time.

Q. If I am sensitive to impressions, does that mean that the energy of consciousness is present in me at that time?
J.G.B. Consciousness can be noticed at moments of transition from automatism to sensitivity. There is a moment that we call "waking up." At the moment you wake up, some energy of consciousness acts. But it is only a very, very small quantity not enough to keep the whole process of transformation going and most people overlook its importance and allow the moment to pass unused.

Q. Would it be any use trying to hold on to being sensitive?
J.G.B. Why not? Certainly it is useful. But that by itself won't give you energy of consciousness.

Q. How would one recognize creative energy?
J.G.B. Only by — and I must give a very strange answer to this — only by the **realization of your own nothingness**. When there is a real consciousness of our own nothingness, not just a state of depression, we can come under the action of the third gradation of cosmic energy. In front of that creative energy, we are really nothing; and therefore, as soon as it appears in us it becomes obvious to us that we are nothing at all. But I must warn you that many people think that they have had the experience of their own nothingness, when they have had some unpleasant shock and are a bit depressed. It is not the same thing. Also, as I said just now, all that we can be aware of is the **result**: creativity transforming automatism into consciousness.

Q. It seems to be such a positive scale — one good thing leading to another good thing — what about the creation of negative things? For instance, is there any E3 in malignant diseases?

J.G.B. I said there is the degeneration as well as transformation, katabolism as well as anabolism. It is possible to say that all disease comes from the action of energies on the wrong level. It is quite true that if a very high energy acts on a low level — without the proper apparatus for transforming it — it may not only produce disease, it might even immediately kill.

Q. You said, at the beginning, that all transformations of energy took place at a price, but you did not mention the price in your two examples.
J.G.B. Of course I did! I said, you have to lose your feeling of "I." Isn't that a price? Wait until you have to do it. It is a big price.

Q. How is it that we must understand these transformations in terms of triads? It seems to me, in connection with chlorophyll, that you have five energies which work at a point. It seems as if it is one energy acting on another producing three others, or several others.
J.G.B. That means there are several actions of different kinds. I also showed in the diagram that there is one part that goes through unchanged. In every one of these diagrams the transformation is only of a part, and there is a very big law in that. Always there has to be division into three. Part goes up, part degenerates, and part remains the same. It can be said that there are "anabolic triads," "katabolic triads," and "stationary triads."

Q. Last week I asked you about the relationship between quantity, quality, and intensity. What I was trying to ask was, what is the ratio of the relationship between quantity, quality, and intensity? Can you use the apparatus to change all of these? I am not quite clear what you mean.
J.G.B. First, about quantity: you can understand this from what I have just been saying about the partition. There is not any change in the total **quantity** because energy is indestructible. All changes of quantity are simply separation, part going right, part going left,

part going up, part going down, part remaining the same. But the total amount is unchanged. That is the principle of the **indestructibility of energy**. The **intensity** of energy in these transformations is very largely a matter of determining whether the transformation can take place at all. You may have the energy of the right kind, but if the intensity is not enough, then nothing happens. For example, there is always a certain amount of energy of consciousness present in us, but unless it becomes intense enough, unless it reaches a certain intensity, nothing happens at all. That is the relationship there. It is the condition of whether the action takes place or does not take place. It is like what I said last week about boiling an egg. Boiling an egg is a process of energy transformation. It is very simple. The change that takes place in the energies of the egg has to do with its possibility of becoming a food. But what is required to transform it is a certain intensity of heat, not too little, not too much.

Now, for the other part of your question. You speak of apparatuses. That really is the most important thing I wanted you all to see. In every single one of these examples, the energies have to be brought together under definite conditions. The example I gave of Maxwell's sorting demon requires a particular apparatus. If such an apparatus could be made to work efficiently, then we should no longer be dependent on any outside source of energy. Again, look at the second example. All the time, in the world, all over the earth, there is carbon dioxide in the air, there is water vapour in the air, and there is sunlight. It falls on everything, but a most extraordinarily constructed apparatus is required before there can be the photosynthesis of carbohydrates. No one could have invented this; it is a hundred million times more extraordinary than any apparatus any man has ever devised. There are many things we can do only by copying the wonderful apparatuses nature uses for her transformations. It is the same with the transformation of food in man. I show you a general diagram, and you must understand, when it is worked out in detail, that each variety in the quality of food requires to be worked on by a particular active element in a particular order. The food has to be brought into a special state of fluidity at which it is able to pass through the apertures in the lining of the intestinal tract that are precisely regulated to allow just that and nothing else to pass through. And it is not only these physical apparatuses — you must understand that the apparatus for self-remembering is even more extraordinary. It is a real miracle. How could one ever suppose that some kind of animal could arise on earth that is able to remember itself? And, what's more, not being able to remember itself because it is automatically made so, as perhaps angels are, but that can find out how to produce a state of self-remembering through its own voluntary efforts. Here again, a special apparatus is needed to make this possible.

✣

LECTURE III

How Energies Do Their Work

EVERY FUNCTION, EVERY ACTIVITY, wherever it may occur, in non-living, living, and universal situations, requires the consumption of energy. Every kind of change is a transformation of energies. But although every function uses energy, no function can use all the energy supplied to it. This rule is universal, but it is not yet properly understood. We know it in the Second Law of Thermodynamics according to which every irreversible transformation of energy must involve some "waste." On the other hand, the First Law tells us that there can be no waste. The solution of the contradiction comes with understanding that, in all energy transformations, three distinct effects occur. One part of the energy supplied for use in an apparatus is consumed in the process itself. A second part is released for a more general purpose. The third part effects some change in the apparatus itself. For example, when our bodies work, they produce heat as well as movement and the heat makes good the loss that is constantly accruing. In addition, the movement strengthens the muscles, and it may improve our skill or efficiency in performing the function in question.

In a very general way, this division always applies. This explains Gurdjieff's saying that when we make efforts we divide the *omnipresent substance okidanokh* into three parts: one is used in the

49

effort, a second serves a general cosmic purpose, while the third can be retained for our own benefit.

For this desirable result to be obtained, the right energy must be supplied in the right quantity and of the right intensity. In the case of our human functions, this requires knowledge of man in four different aspects:

1. Man as an engine for performing mechanical work.
2. Man as a living organism.
3. Man as a centre of personal experience.
4. Man as a cosmic apparatus for the transformation of energy.

THE HUMAN ENGINE

The human body is a heat engine and a machine for doing mechanical work. All our bodily activity depends upon this aspect of our nature. The Human Engine works with the three lowest energies: heat (E12), directed energy (E11), and connected energy (E10). Our body can be regarded as a complicated system of heat engines, made up of various levers which work through our bones and cartilages, together with the muscles and all the various pipes or tubes through which different liquids flow. These include not only our veins and arteries, but all the many vessels and passages through which the body fluids are constantly being pumped. This system is an engine governed by exactly the same laws as any other engine, such as a steam engine, or any mechanical device that we may use for producing mechanical results, such as a lever or a pump.

The working of our bodies requires that they be maintained within narrow limits of temperature. The limits are narrower with man than for other animals, no doubt because the human organism has to perform far more complex and delicately adjusted functions. The foundation of our physical existence is **heat**: that is, E12. The motive power that keeps our limbs and the body fluids

in constant movement, in order to be able to adapt to the working
of the higher energies, is of exactly the same kind that makes any
other heat engine work: that is, expansion and contraction of
fluids as heat is put into them and heat is taken out of them. The
mechanical energy by which our bodies are able to function as
heat engines is the directed energy, E11. That which preserves the
form and structure of our bodies — our skeleton, our muscles, our
blood vessels — that is what I called in the first lecture the
connected energy, E10. It is the energy that enables things to be
what they are. It enables tables to be tables, it enables a hand to be
a hand, bone to be bone, muscle to be muscle, and so on. The

TABLE 6
THE ENGINES OF THE BODY

Adaptation and Adjustment		Plastic Energy	E9
Solid engines	Liquid engines		
Bones & cartilage as levers	Heart and circulation, lymphatic system of pumps and tubes	Connected Energy	E10
Motive power of muscles and pumps		Directed Energy	E11
Bodily heat		Dispersed Energy	E12

adaptability of the human frame — from our mobile limbs to the most complex adjustments of the organs of perception and action — all depend upon the properties of the plastic energy, E9.

It is a good thing to remember that the foundation of our existence is a heat engine like all other heat engines, only more complicated than most. Sometimes it is even valuable to study this engine as such; that is, without reference to any of the vital functions by which it is moved. We do this by bringing in front of our mental vision our anatomy, in its aspect as a system of levers, pipes, and pumps.

A second, scarcely less characteristic, feature of the human body is its relation to gravity. We stand erect in the gravitational field of the earth and this maintains in us a constant flow of directed energy. If our postures are defective, this flow is interrupted. We cannot observe the consequences directly; but they build up until malfunctioning of the whole system produces pathological conditions in the vital energies. The trouble can be diagnosed upon the level of the connected energy — that is, the skeletal and muscular structure — as has been shown by F. M. Alexander, Ida Rolf, Moshe Feldenkrais, and others who have worked upon the gravitational influences that act on the body.

MAN AS A LIVING ORGANISM

We now pass to the four energies by which life is sustained and all the vital functions are performed. These are E8, Constructive; E7, Vital; E6, Automatic; and E5, Sensitive Energy. These four energies have a common property that can be called **autokinesis**, or the power of self-induced movement. This power varies enormously over the range from movement produced by a pattern (constructive) to movement produced as a elective response (sensitive). All through the range, we have before us modes of existence that are not wholly mechanical. Even the simplest self-reproducing protein is something more than a machine inasmuch as it moves itself. "Self-movingness" is not only the locomotive power of a heat engine, but the self-adaptiveness of the body, and is the foundation of animal life.

The plastic energy, E9, which dominates the body viewed as an engine, is now seen as the foundation of life processes. It occupies a transitional place. In its crudest form, it gives flexibility to the body and its limbs and organs. In its finer forms, it gives rise to the colloidal state in which an enormous concentration of energy is available at surfaces thus making possible the intense local energy exchanges that are required by life.

TABLE 7
THE VITAL FUNCTIONS OF THE ORGANISM

The Body as Functional Complex	Automatic Energy	E6
The Vital Processes of the living body, respiration, locomotion, assimilation, regulation	Vital Energy	E7
The Regulative Mechanisms of the blood and nervous system	Constructive Energy	E8
The Power of Locomotion and inner adaptation	Plastic Energy	E9

At the next stage, we encounter the energy by which life builds its own bodies. There is a fundamental difference between the construction of a crystalline form and that of a living body. The former is the crystal itself whereas the body is both the vessel and the instrument of life — but not life itself. The power to make one's own vessel is given by the constructive energy E8. This is not vital energy E7, but its instrument.

Before we look at the life process as a whole, we must pay some attention to the role of the constructive energy. It builds the body, from food and air, maintains its good functioning, repairs it when it is damaged, and regulates its very complicated working. It can do all this in spite of lacking any power of independent initiative or adaptation. This is possible because it follows a pattern that guides and directs its activity. Every living organism has a pattern, called its genetic constitution, that it receives from its parents. The pattern is virtually complete at the moment the ovum is fertilized. Recent developments in chemistry of proteins suggest that the pattern is associated with very complex substances such as DNA (deoxyribonucleic acid), but that these substances are not themselves the pattern. It seems that biological science is reaching out towards an understanding of the constructive energy and its role in embryology. But its importance is not confined to body-building. It is also responsible for the complicated regulative mechanism that works through special chemical substances and nerve processes. It is constantly adjusting the balance between the needs of all the different parts of the body. It regulates the distribution of the energy that enters the body from the food we eat and from the air we breathe. The energies that keep this special mechanism going are a special class of the constructive energies, E8. Sometimes they act by breaking down complex substances like proteins into simpler forms; sometimes they act by building these simple forms into elaborate structures that are required for repairing the tissues of our bodies. They also regulate the temperature and chemical state of our blood within very narrow limits. The whole system forms the **vital regulative mechanism**, as distinct from what we shall come to later; that is, the psychic regulative mechanism.

I said just now that the constructive energy has no power of innovation or adaptation. It works by what is called "self-optimizing feedback" which, as students of cybernetics know, means the ability to maintain a pre-set pattern in spite of external disturbances and in this way to move towards a pre-determined objective or goal.

In cybernetics, the pattern is called a programme and it can be adjusted only by the operator or "programmer." Life needs a similar arrangement and this is provided by the vital energy E7. The fundamental character of the vital energy consists in its power of adaptation and self-regulation, not just to maintain its existence but to reach a goal that is not predetermined but constantly requiring adjustment according to circumstances. The "goal-seeking" activity that characterizes all forms of life cannot be sustained by constructive energy alone. We have, therefore, to postulate the existence of a higher form of energy: that is **life itself**.

Life uses the organism. Life has its goals and purposes and uses the organism to realize them. This peculiar power of getting beyond the immediate situation is a fundamental property that distinguishes living from non-living forms. It is associated with the property of "inner connectedness" that leads from unconscious to conscious energies.

While E8 and E9 are always below the threshold of our awareness, the highest vital energy, E7, stands at the dividing point between what we can be directly aware of and what we can observe only in its outward results. We can put it this way: that from the E7 upwards, all the energies can be experienced from **inside** — from E7 downwards all the energies can be experienced only from **outside**. Vitality stands at the transition between the two. If the higher energies in man function normally, they are able to keep contact with the state of vitality of the organism. This can be called "awareness of oneself as a living animal." Upon the supply of the vital energy E7, our state of normal organic activity depends. There are various means by which deficiency of this energy can be remedied. Some of these are used by physicians, others by what are called "faith-healers." But it is necessary to know the consequences of using these means, because supplying some energy of the quality E7 artificially can seriously disturb the regulative mechanism. Perhaps only long afterwards the consequences are seen in the degeneration of some part of the regulative mechanism.

THE PSYCHIC FUNCTIONS

Human life can be seen as a threefold relationship of time, space, and eternity. Each of these three "determining conditions" is experienced through corresponding instruments which can also be called "centres of functioning" or brains. Our connection with time is made by thought, our connection with space is made by sensation, and with eternity by feeling.

Animals, which have only rudimentary intellectual centres, have almost no awareness of time. They have highly developed sensations and are thereby well adapted to space. The higher mammals and birds have the emotional centre and are able to experience distinctions of like and dislike, pleasure and pain that are associated with the eternal pattern of their natures.

This leads to a simplified notion of human nature as a constantly changing pattern of relationships between thought, feeling, and sensation. This pattern is sometimes called the "psyche" or "selfhood." The three centres or brains which comprise the content of the psyche normally work with the two higher life energies, automatic E6 and sensitive E5; but under favourable conditions they can be raised to a higher level of working by the conscious energy E4. Beyond the psychic functions, there are the so-called "Higher Centres" that work with a blend of conscious E4 and creative E3 energies. We have the scheme of Table 8:

TABLE 8
THE HUMAN PSYCHE

Supra-Conscious Inspiration or the "Higher Self"	Creative Energy	E3
The Intellectual or Conscious level of the centres	Conscious Energy	E4
The Emotional or Reactional level of the centres	Sensitive Energy	E5
The Mechanical level of Function	Automatic Energy	E6

THE "BRAINS" OR CENTRES OF FUNCTION

In 1921, when P. D. Ouspensky first taught the psychological system and methods of Gurdjieff in London, the idea that man is a "three-brained being" was new and surprising. Progress in experimental psychology since then has made the idea much more plausible. We have also a much better understanding of subconscious and supraconscious regions of the human psyche than obtained when analytical psychology was founded. Less importance is attached now to "complexes" and more to "mechanisms" and "structures" associated with the different functions. The many books that have been written on Gurdjieff, his teaching and his methods have made people aware of such fundamental notions as that "man is asleep, "man has no I," "man is a machine," and "man cannot do." Such statements, which were startling and controversial forty years ago, are in keeping not only with scientific thinking, but with current thinking generally. We have more sober views of what man is and what he can do than those which prevailed at the beginning of this century; but we are also more inclined to accept Gurdjieff's doctrine of individual transformism or the potentiality of man for immense psychic and spiritual development. Nevertheless, confusion still surrounds many of Gurdjieff's psychological ideas — partly because of the multiplicity of interpreters, and partly because he himself avoided like the plague any fixed presentation that might encourage his pupils to believe that they were in possession of the "last word" about man and his nature. There is, however, a deeper and more positive reason for apparently incompatible statements, such as:

Unlike animals, which have two, or even only one brain; man is a three-brained being.

Man has three centres for his bodily, feeling, and intellectual functions.

Man has four centres: instinctive, moving, emotional, and intellectual.

Man has five centres, the fifth being the sex centre.

Man has seven centres, of which two — the higher emotional and the higher mental — are beyond his ordinary consciousness.

Man is a three-brained being and can never be otherwise; but he can attain to an unspecified number of "gradations of objective reason," each of which endows him with some supranormal power.

According to Gurdjieff, all these statements are valid, providing we can assign them to the right perspective. In some cases, this is straightforward. For example, the "first brain" has two parts, one which controls the inner, instinctive processes and the other the external or voluntary movements. For many purposes, the two parts can be studied as separate "brains." For our present purpose — that is, for the study of energies as fuels — we can take the three brains as three machines performing different functions, but giving different results according to the kind of fuel supplied to them. You can look upon the situation as the combination of nine possibilities. I shall represent the three centres by the letters "I" for

Intellectual, "E" for Emotional, and "M" for Moving-Instinctive. The three energies are" A" for Automatic E6, "S" for Sensitive E5, and "C" for Conscious E4.

TABLE 9
ENERGIES AND FUNCTIONS

Energies	Functions or Powers		
	Moving	Emotional	Intellectual
Conscious	M x C	E x C	I x C
Sensitive	M x S	E x S	I x S
Automatic	M x A	E x A	I x A

It is possible to have any combination of these nine working together or separately. Thus, we can have conscious working of the Moving Centre combined with automatic thought and sensitive emotion. This happens at moments of bodily danger when the body performs incredible acrobatic feats to save itself and the thinking brain does not become aware of the danger until after it has passed. There is an accompanying emotional excitement from which the action is "seen" though not "thought."

There are scores of possible combinations, but only a few of these play an active part in our everyday life. Most people live predominantly upon the automatic level of functioning and their sensitivity remains in a dream state, receiving impressions from sensation and thought, but out of touch with their behaviour.

This is not how man should be living. You must remember that we have already passed beyond the ready-made machines that keep vegetative and animal life going, to the study of functions whose very nature is to be self-directing. There are much greater differences in the working of centres than in the work of the vital mechanism. Whereas the bodily engines always work in the same way, the working of our psychic centres changes quite sharply as they pass from the action of one quality of energy to that of another. Only the mechanical functions that are supplied with the automatic energy are always in action. The automatic functioning of our thinking and feeling and of our instinctive and moving centres is the foundation of our everyday life. Only under some special stimulus do we use the higher energies and so produce the change in functioning that they can give. That stimulus can either come **accidentally** from outside, or it can come **intentionally** from within ourselves.

We have the means of studying in ourselves the working of the third triad of energies. We must learn to recognize the presence of each of these three energies in ourselves. We have also to learn how to bring in the two higher energies when they are needed for the purpose of changing the quality of the working of one or all of our functions. For example, when one of the centres begins to work with sensitive energy, a portion of sensitivity arises in that centre. Thus, with sensitive energy, we not only associate words and images but we begin to realize that we are only associating. This is possible because something more than the association of the moment is present. That "something" connects the association either with past memories or previously made decisions, or with some external impression that we are receiving at that moment. If sensitive energy E5 is not present in the centre, we do not **notice** at all. Our associations then go on and on without our noticing them. That is the automatic or mechanical state of the man-machine. Automatic mental association plays so great a part in our lives, that Gurdjieff gave it a special name: **formating**. He called the automatic part of the thinking centre the "formatory apparatus."

The same automaticity is seen in each of the other centres. Our feeling state is constantly fluctuating — it is the result of the combination of all the different psychic impulses that are acting upon us. Everything that affects our thoughts, or our bodies, produces an automatic response in our feeling centre. All that we notice is the resulting state of pleasure or no-pleasure, interest or boredom, excitement or the lack of it — we are not sensitive to the sources of our state. Lack of sensitiveness characterizes the work of all the centres when the motive power is only the automatic energy, E6.

STATES OF CONSCIOUSNESS

When the sensitive energy begins to flow, it is sometimes called the **first moment of waking**. A particular quality of work comes from a particular centre so long as that sensitive energy flows. As soon as the flow of sensitive energy stops the work of the centre reverts to the automatic mental associations, automatic feeling states, automatic bodily movements, and so on.

The full output of the centres is obtained only when there is a supply of conscious energy. The production of conscious energy E4 depends upon a certain intentional action connected with impressions. The E4 made unintentionally is used up in maintaining the transformation of E6 to E5 for the purposes of the organism. In the ordinary way, there is no surplus energy E4 available for the work of the centres. So, in the ordinary way, man knows nothing about the work of the centres that is possible with the help of conscious energy. Such small quantities of conscious energy as are produced in us are used up in the organism, and nothing is left over for any conscious thinking or conscious feeling or conscious movement.

If we wish to understand something of the true potentialities of our psychic functions, we must realize that there is no way of obtaining from our centres their full possible work unless there is a supply of the two higher kinds of energy. Everyone, with even a little experience of self-observation and of the study of centres, knows how very little it is possible to be in the sensitive state — the state in which we **notice** what is happening. This can be called the half-waking state. It is quite impossible — though people do not realize it — to be in the full-waking state without the conscious energy, E4.

It can be said of the ordinary life of man, that he lives nearly the whole of his life with his psychic functions working only with automatic energy, E6. Very occasionally, as a result of involuntary shocks, a certain amount of energy of E5 enters and then one or another of his centres half wakes up. It is extremely rare — it may happen two or three times in a lifetime — that there is a sufficient supply of energy E4 released to give him the experience of conscious working of his centres. At the same time it is possible for man so to increase both the supply of E5 and E4 that he can produce, whenever it is needed, the higher quality of work of the centres.

What is meant by this higher quality working? I have said a little about sensitivity and what I called the **half-awake state**. This is the state in which one sees that a different kind of life is possible for us. If that half-awake state appears in one centre only — that means if a higher energy has gone only into one centre, the thinking or the moving centre — there is scarcely any power to make use of the possibility which is seen. One may imagine that one is doing something intentional at the moment that one comes to this half-awake state but what one does is no more than the result of something that has gone beforehand. It is not really the free use of the possibility that is present at that moment. That is very hard to grasp and to accept in oneself. Even when we come to the half-awake state which is given by the sensitive psychic energy, all that happens to us is that we have a different kind of reaction. Our reaction becomes connected with some previous intention or previous decision, or with some point of view established in us, instead of being quite accidental. But it is not free.

Without consciousness, there is no free power in any of our centres. We cannot think what we wish to think, we cannot feel what we wish to feel, or obtain from our bodies anything intentional except through the fourth, the highest, life energy E4.

You remember in the last lecture, when I spoke about the transformation of energies, I said that to transform E5 into E4 intentionally in ourselves, it is necessary to pay a high price. Because we do not see that we have no power of doing anything of ourselves in the absence of the conscious energy, we do not readily find in ourselves the need to make that sacrifice, or to pay the price of having that energy.

One important difference between what is called **full awakening** of the centres, when there is the E4 energy present, and the **half-awake** state when there is E5, is that the conscious energy brings **all** the centres together. The E5 only brings about awakening in one centre; that is, one centre becomes sensitive while the other centres remain asleep unless some E5 goes independently into them also. But when there is E4, when there is conscious energy, **all the centres wake up together.** Under the motive power of E4, a man simultaneously thinks and feels and experiences his body all as one single moment of experience.

Unfortunately the machine of our organism is not prepared to stand the intensity of experience that belongs to E4 and therefore in the normal harmonious development of man it is necessary to pass through the stage of half-awakening of each of the centres — that is, the stage at which the flow of E5 into the centres becomes sufficient for the half-awake state to occur quite often in all the centres. You will realize that very much of the work that we do with our movements[3], with our exercises, with our practice of attention, and so on, is concerned with the preparation of our functions to stand eventually the intensity of the working that comes when we are able to liberate the flow of E4.

THE CREATIVE ENERGY

Conscious and sensitive energy combine to produce the

various states of consciousness to which we are accustomed. They can be called the "Content of the Mind." The automatic energy is below the level of our awareness and its action can be called unconscious, or better, subconscious. Now, psychologists have realized that there are also sources of action in us that are not conscious and yet are not subconscious. Jung has referred to a "supraconscious" by which man is connected with universal forms. This supraconscious is nothing less than the creative energy. Its action has an inexplicable character, not only because it is beyond consciousness but chiefly because it is not subject to the limitations of time and place as we know them. When it works in us, we ascribe it to chance, spontaneity, good luck, inspiration, or, following Gurdjieff, to the working of the *Higher Intellectual Centre.* Gurdjieff's diagram is as follows:

TABLE 10
THE SEVEN CENTRES ACCORDING TO
GURDJIEFF

Mental		Higher Intellectual
Emotional		Higher Emotional
Instinctive	Sex	Moving

I have found it useful to show the working of the four energies as a tetrad in the form of a cross (see Figure 8):

The horizontal line represents the conscious life or the "mind." The vertical line gives the three levels of functioning. The oblique connections show how the four energies combine to produce all the different manifestations of human experience. I shall return to all this in the next lecture.

FIG. 8
THE FOUR ENERGIES IN MAN'S ACTIVITY

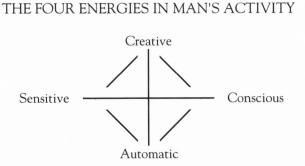

INTEGRATION OF THE FUNCTIONS

Much of our work is concerned with bringing the centres to use the qualities of energy that can give the results required for any particular purpose. That preparation of the centres and the **making of the connections** by which the different energies can flow into the centres is different from the work of the **transformation** of energy through the action of one energy on another, that I spoke about earlier. Both are necessary, but it is useless to carry the transformations of energy to a high degree and produce energies of the E5 and E4 qualities — that is, sensitive and conscious energies — in amounts exceeding what the centres are prepared to work with. Therefore, it is also necessary to bring our centres as frequently as possible into the half-waking or sensitive state which is the real preparation for the full waking state that comes when the conscious energy is liberated. But I warn you that the converse is also true. It is useless to work only on training the centres if the necessary energy for higher level working is not going to be available. Methods which consist only in training the functions lead to very little if the centres can only be supplied with automatic energy and such quantities of sensitive energy as are made in the ordinary processes of our experience. We can translate this into psychological language, by saying that it is no use trying to work very much on improving the work of our centres unless we also work on self-remembering, which is the condition for producing in ourselves an increased output of the E5 energy. Unless we work also on the transmutation of our egoism, which is the condition for liberating in ourselves the E4 energy, we cannot have consciousness of all our functions.

The energies of the highest group fall outside the scope of the present lecture. They cannot be described as "fuels" and we cannot "use" them. On the contrary, it is they that use us and it is we that are "fuel" or "food" for them. There are different ways of being used and the understanding of these differences is the key to all other understanding. I shall devote the whole of the last lecture to this question.

✛

QUESTIONS

Q. If one does not do movements, can the moving centre still be properly prepared to receive the conscious energy — or must it be dealt with in some other way?

J.G.B. The training of the moving centre, like the other centres, consists in bringing it into what I call the half-awake state. This is done by bringing sensitive energy into the work of the moving centre. It is not indispensable to have special exercises for that. For example, it is possible to bring sensitive energy into the ordinary customary movements of our body, such as walking, or speaking. If we begin to listen and experience the vibrations of sound as we speak, that already is bringing sensitive energy to the instinctive centre. If, when we walk we are able to become sensitive to the process of walking, we sensitize the moving centre. Special exercises are for facilitating this, but they are not indispensable. Through becoming sensitive to one's postures and gestures, one brings the moving centre into the half-awake state.

Q. Where does the nervous system come into this?
J.G.B. It is connected with the regulative mechanism that is in the central position in the animal diagram. It is the work of E8.

Q. How can one bring sensitive energy into the feeling and thinking centres?
J.G.B. The difference between automatic and sensitive thinking is this. With automatic thinking, we are not aware of the **meaning** of what we are thinking. For example, if we are speaking, and if what we say is coming from the automatic thinking, what we **mean** by what we say does not matter to us. We just speak. It is a reaction. As soon as you begin to ask yourself, **as you are speaking**, "But what do I mean as I am saying this?", then you realize it is necessary to be more sensitive. Maybe you find you have not got the power of attention that enables you to be sensitive to the meaning of what you are saying while you are saying it, or to the meaning of what you are thinking while you are thinking it. But when you begin to practice that, when you try — as you use a word — to become sensitive to the meaning of the word that you are using, you are already beginning to work with the second part of the thinking centre.

The bringing of sensitive energy to the feeling centre is quite different. There is in the thinking centre the power to direct the sensitive energy into the feelings, but that is only possible when there is some conscious energy in the thinking centre. Then the thinking centre has power over the feelings. It is then able to **direct** the feelings as it wishes. Otherwise the bringing of sensitive energy to the feeling centre can only be an indirect result of the combined action of the thinking and moving centres. One can discover that whenever one sets oneself with determination to work with two centres, and particularly with the head and the body, one finds that one has, by that act, become sensitive in one's feelings. That is the **indirect** way. The direct way is only possible when there is a supply of conscious energy in the thinking centre.

Q. What part has attention in this?
J.G.B. Attention is not an energy. It is a power of the will. We are not speaking now about the will and the various powers of the will. One difficulty with us is, of course, that we have not only an insufficient supply of energy but, what is much worse, we have almost no will. Attention is the simplest and perhaps the most primitive of all the powers of the will. We know only too well how little of that power we have.

Q. You promised at the first lecture to mention something about **time**, about the duration of energies. There is an enormous difference between a flash of consciousness and the sensitive state. How is it possible to prolong this state of awakening consciousness?
J.G.B. There is our own subjective time. Each one of us has his own time. *That* time depends entirely upon the quality of our experience. it has nothing to do with clocks or with the turning of the earth on its axis. It has only to do with the quality of our experience. You have no doubt read in *All and Everything* about those unfortunate beings — men living on the earth — how the duration of their existence is constantly shortening. The meaning of that is simple: it is that the **quality of our experience deteriorates.** Therefore the amount of time that people have grows less

and less. Some people in the course of hours may live more than other people in a whole lifetime. The times for different people are quite different, and the times of the different parts of centres are again quite different. More happens with one minute of sensitive energy in a centre than in twenty-four hours of automatic energy. Far more happens in one second with conscious energy than with hours of sensitive energy. Creative energy is not subject to the laws of time and space as we know them.

So you must understand that you cannot speak about the duration of things just by what is measured by the clock. Somebody asked at the first lecture how the higher energies are related to time. The three higher energies are outside the laws of time. At any given moment there is a whole lifetime of experience or perhaps even a thousand lifetimes of experience in these higher energies. As soon as anyone comes into contact with these higher energies, they are set free from time in the ordinary sense.

Q. In other words, that kind of experience is never lost.
J.G.B. It is never lost. That is so.

Q. I want to ask which category you put the energy which drove people such as Shakespeare, Mozart, Beethoven — the geniuses who wrote works which are imperishable, outside of normal experience. Is it consciousness, or is it something higher? I do not know where to place it. I know it is exceptional, but it is human.
J.G.B. Occasionally the creative energy enters into some people's lives. But one must realize that all these geniuses produce very little that is truly of a higher order. How much did Beethoven produce of music that was not explainable in terms of conscious or even sensitive energy? Not very much. And the same with Shakespeare. In Shakespeare's plays there is only a very small amount of what is of a truly creative quality. Creative power is not something that works all the time. The rest is achieved with technique. When there is true creation, it comes from beyond consciousness — from the Creative Energy E3.

Q. Do I understand that our emotions are altered by a predeter-mined mechanical decision to alter them? Do I understand from what you said that only consciousness in our thinking centre can change our emotions, and that, if we imagine that we are changing our emotions at the present time, it is that we have made a decision — a pre-decision — to alter our emotional state, and that is what is actually occurring?

J.G.B. Certainly in any case our emotions are very much depen-dent upon the restraining of our automatic reactions. It is almost impossible for most people to have any sensitivity in their emo-tional life. The emotional life of man is the most insensitive of all. Man seldom has any voluntary power over his emotional life. But, of course, we do automatize various reactions — there is no special difficulty with the restraint of automatic emotions, automatic reactions, such as no longer flying into a temper if something irritates us. So-called "control" is no more than the automatic conditioning which is going on in us all the time. But people call that "controlling." When you begin really seriously to study your own emotional life, and especially if people are prepared to under-take this together to some extent, you will be astonished when you discover the extent to which we are all **emotionally** insensitive. And it is extraordinary how people live in imagination about that.

Q How can I increase the sensitive state in myself? There seems to be a moment of possibility. How can I make myself more sensitive? Is it a question of more relaxation? There seems to be just a moment when I can go on and there is consciousness there.

J.G.B. The first thing to grasp is that nearly all the time our functions work automatically. It is difficult to grasp this because we mistake the automatic instinctive reactions, emotional reactions, and mental reactions for true sensitivity One example can show this: sensitive energy can distinguish between the affirming and denying aspects of a given stimulus. The automatic energy does not: it reacts either to the plus or to the minus, either by pleasure or by pain, or by yes or by no. But the sensitive energy feels both.

One way in which one can begin to increase one's own sensitivity is whenever one experiences the negative to try to experience also the positive, and whenever one experiences the positive to experi- ence also the negative. That is, if one dislikes something, to look for what in one also likes it. If sensitive energy is available, one will find that there is something in one that likes it as well as dislikes it. If I say "yes" to some idea, that is only my automatic energies, because automatic working of my thinking centre can do that. As soon as my thinking begins to be sensitive, what I say "yes" to I also say "no" to. When I begin to come under such a combined action of "yes" and "no," I am half-awake and there is the possibility then for me to come to something more, which is to be free from both yes and no. This is only possible with the conscious energy E4.

Once we realize the nature of automatic functions, we can recognize what is meant by the separation of consciousness and sensitivity. This is the condition of true self-observation as distinct from thinking about oneself. In Gurdjieff's language, it is the *first conscious shock*. This is the real secret of increasing sensitivity.

Q. I do not understand about half-waking, and being fully awake. If we experience conscious energy would part of our being still remain unconscious?
J.G.B. Yes, certainly, there is always a great part of our nature that works permanently below the threshold of awareness. Don't forget that the vital and constructive energies are always at work. Also, at the automatic level, a constant activity is maintained in the nervous system, including the cortex.

Q. What is the difference between that activity and the half-awake state?
J.G.B. In the half-awake state you **feel** yourself awake. When you really are awake, you **see** what it is to be asleep. The chief difference is this, that when there is conscious energy we have an awareness of the whole. The diagram of Figure 8 shows that, when the conscious energy is added, the centre sees the whole of our

functions in perspective; it sees the half-awake state of the centres by which each one of them is able to have its own characteristic experience. But it also sees the automaton, because the automatic part always continues.

³The system of rhythmic movements taught by G. I. Gurdjieff.

❖

LECTURE IV

The Secret Of Creativity

I N THE LAST LECTURE, I showed you how the twelve energies are
connected with the four principal states or levels of existence in
which man can have a place. Tonight, I am going to ask you to
concentrate your attention upon the four energies that govern
creative activity in man. I am devoting a whole lecture to this
subject because creativity is the property or power that entitles
man to the proud title, "Made in the Image of God." Man would
be wholly subject to natural laws and his life and possible evolution
would be wholly dependent upon external forces, if he had no
power of creative action by which influences from a higher level
could enter human life and initiate changes of direction on every
scale from that of individual fulfillment to that of the total history
of mankind.

In our study of the four triads of energy, I referred to the
Creative Energy as the power by which all existence is maintained
and suggested that we are constantly under its action, although we
cannot be aware of it. I am now going to approach the subject from
a different angle — that of our activity as beings who are capable of
creative action. For this, we shall take the three energies that
maintain our psychic functions — automatic, sensitive, and conscious — and add the creative energy as a fourth. In this way, we
pass from the triad to the tetrad; but the present tetrad is different

73

from those which I used in the first lecture to derive the twelve orders or kinds of energy.

THE TETRAD

The tetrad can be represented by the symbol of the cross. The vertical limb represents the ascending and descending processes of creation and the horizontal limb the instruments by which creation is made possible. There are four more connections between the four extremities. Each of these can be interpreted as a necessary part of the total creative action we are trying to understand.

FIG. 9
THE TETRAD OF CREATIVE ACTIVITY

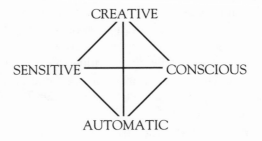

SENSITIVITY AND CONSCIOUSNESS

This diagram can be related directly to human activity. The horizontal line represents what we call our "conscious experience" or just "consciousness." People — even psychologists — commonly overlook the fact that consciousness has two distinct components corresponding to sensitive energy E5 and Conscious Energy E4. These two energies combine to bridge the gap between life and existence beyond life. The one (E5) enables us to be aware of the processes of life in our psychic functions, but the other (E4) enables us to be aware of ourselves. Whereas life is dependent upon processes or functions to maintain itself, the universal existence is self-sufficient or self-dependent. We men derive our characteristic quality of self-sufficiency from the presence in us of conscious energy. Unfortunately, in the ordinary state of man, the conscious energy is absorbed by the sensitive energy like water is absorbed by a sponge — although a sponge is coarser than water — and the true nature of consciousness is lost to view. When sensitivity and consiousness are not held apart, we have no direct contact with the higher part of our nature. In terms of actual experience we can say that, in the ordinary way, man can be aware of what is going on, but he is not conscious of being aware of what is going on. Sometimes he does involuntarily divide E5 from E4, and then he is aware that there is something in him other than the activity of his sensitivity.

THE SENSITIVE SCREEN

I want here to introduce a convenient image — I will not call it a hypothesis because there is no need to consider whether it is "true" or not — to help you to picture the way the sensitive energy works. In the last lecture, I referred to it as the "emotional parts of centres"; but said that this is a misleading term used by Ouspensky to describe the state in which we are aware of our functional activity without controlling it. Another way of picturing it is to look upon the sensitive energy as a kind of screen upon which images are thrown. These images can come through the senses — sight, hearing, touch, and so on — or from one of the centres — thought images, feeling images, etc., or from the store of memories and habits. From any one of these sources, images can be projected onto the sensitivity to produce what is sometimes called the "flow of thought" or the "stream of consciousness." The point is that they appear and disappear involuntarily; though under certain circumstances we can produce them at will. These "circumstances" are connected with the conscious energy (E4) and they correspond to the state called "self-consciousness."

The sensitive screen I have just described is that which is commonly called the **mind**. We speak of thoughts and images being "in the mind"; but the point is that they are "on" the screen when we are aware of them.

We use, strangely enough, the word self-consciousness in two different senses, both of which are quite right, and the difference between them is that one is voluntary and the other involuntary. Involuntary self-consciousness is the state of acute embarrassment that we feel when we are aware that our sensitivity (E5) is out of our own control. In this state our behaviour continues to produce images on our sensitivity without our being able to control them. We feel awkward, and very often this produces various physiological changes in the body, such as blushing. That kind of self-consciousness is certainly one of separation between the conscious and the sensitive energies. We are well aware in that state that there is something in us which is sensitive and something that is conscious of our sensitivity. But this condition does not lead us very far, because when it arises, there is no control over the situation — in fact, it really is an awareness of our inability to control what is going on, on the sensitive level. The other state is totally different, for it is brought about by the intentional separation between the consciousness and the sensitivity. This intentional act produces a state of consciousness of self, in which we are able to stand apart and observe what is going on in the sensitivity. Then we even have a possibility of directing and controlling it.

The important thing, at this moment, is that you should see for yourselves whether you can recognize that there are in fact two distinct states in us, which are sometimes merged and sometimes separated: one a state of **sensitivity** and the other a state of **consciousness**. Only you yourselves can know for certain that your consciousness is usually carried along by your sensitivity d there is not an inner detachment or observing of what is going on. The merging of consciousness and sensitivity produces a state in which there is no power to alter what is happening. In that state, we fall under the control of the automatism; that is, of the automatic energy E6 working through the nervous system like a vast electronic computer.

SOLVING PROBLEMS

Suppose that we want to understand some problem presented to us from outside by someone else speaking to us. It reaches us through the senses, but it may also arise somewhere from our own memories of the past, or a combination of the two. In any case, it enters our awareness by the path that leads from the automatism to the sensitivity, because the automatism is connected to the out-side world through the senses. It is also connected to our own past experiences through memories and habits. The automatism is like the counter from which we go and buy whatever we need from the "shop," which is the world of sense experience present and past.

Let us suppose that some problem has been presented to our sensitivity. At this point, we either accept or reject it. Either it interests us and we wish to find an answer, or it does not interest us and our sensitivity fails to respond to it. Then new impressions and memories drive it out of our awareness. But supposing that this problem arouses in us some reaction of interest and the desire to find a solution to it. What usually happens then is that the problem remains as a series of mental images, on the screen of the sensitivity, which then recalls from the automatism various impressions of the past — that is, memories — part of which it may do quite without being aware of it, due to automatic ways of thinking to which we have become habituated, so that we call on them without even noticing it. Or we may recall particular facts, as we call them from our store of memories, or else we seek for information from outside by reading, by studying, by asking questions, and so on. In other words, we may try to solve this problem with the help of material that we can call on through our automatic energy (E6). Some problems can be solved adequately by this means alone. In fact, most problems that arise for us from day to day are of the kind that can be solved with the help of our past experience and our knowledge of what is going on around us. When the problem is thrown up, from our sensitivity, of providing food for our bodies because we are hungry, the thought that it is now time for a meal enters the sensitivity. The problem is quickly solved, because we know where to go for a meal and what to do about it.

From time to time, problems arise that cannot be solved in this way. Then it becomes necessary to make connections that the sensitive energy alone is not able to make. The ready-made material that is, as it were, scanned by the sensitivity, fails to provide us with the solution to the problem. It may be necessary to see new connections that we have never seen before. This can only happen if there is a separation between sensitivity and consciousness. This is necessary because the consciousness has certain properties and powers that the sensitivity lacks, and these powers are paralyzed so long as the consciousness is absorbed in the sensitivity. The nature of the sensitive energy is such that it works entirely on a stop-go, yes-no kind of mechanism. If something is presented to it, it can accept it or reject it. As I said before, in the case of problems, the sensitivity can be interested, or not interested, and reject what comes to it. It is presented with possible solutions to the problem and it can say yes or no, like with the problem of food — shall I go to this place or that place, it confronts this with the amount of money I have in my pocket and it says yes or no to it in those kind of simple terms of putting one factor against another, either accepting or rejecting — not always in this factual way, but sometimes in terms of feelings. We may want to go to an expensive restaurant, and know that we cannot afford it; and so between the "I want" and "I can," there is a direct conflict of yes and no, and one or the other will prevail. The sensitive energy can scarcely go beyond comparing things in twos — pairs of feelings like likes and dislikes and so on. It can recognize the "feel" of conflicting stimuli and react to one or the other; but it does not give the power to stand back, reflect and judge.

THE POWER OF CONSCIOUSNESS

Consciousness has a much greater connecting or integrating power. When the conscious energy is really liberated from the stream of awareness, it is able to see many things that apply; according to the degree of freedom to which it can come, it can see more or less. In order to see, one must stand away, otherwise one will not "see the wood for the trees." Such narrowness is typical of the sensitive energy, whereas seeing the whole, "the wood," is characteristic of the conscious energy. There are problems which are intractable on the level of sensitivity, but which can be solved on the level of consciousness. In this state, they are not solved by bringing in anything which was not there before, but by seeing connections, and meanings, and significance, that we did not see before.

When we have the experience of seeing what we did not see a moment ago, a kind of opening of the "inner eye" of the understanding, we can recognize it as the working of consciousness. For this to happen, we must either have a stroke of luck, in that our consciousness liberates itself long enough to produce this condition of integration of the material, or we have to know a means of bringing ourselves into a state where we can stand aside from the problem.

THE LIBERATION OF CONSCIOUSNESS

I must here refer to the well-known practice called "quietening the mind." This consists in allowing the images that arise in the sensitivity to settle down. This method can produce, for a short time, a state of detached consciousness. It can be produced for a much longer time, also with a greater intensity, through various sharper experiences which, for example, may paralyze the working of the sensitive energy. And this kind of paralyzing of the sensitive energy can of course be produced by artificial means, such as narcotics, and that is why, in the various conditions of narcosis there is an enormous increase in the field of vision, inwardly and outwardly, and the sense of integrating, of seeing things as a whole, and especially of seeing meanings, the overwhelming significance of things, such as has been described by everyone who has experimented with narcotics. All of that is really the result of a certain paralyzing, or stopping of the activity of the sensitivity, with the arising of the link between E5 and E4, with that being broken by the action of the narcotic, the sensitivity then no longer imprisons the consciousness in the same way; there is a certain separation of consciousness. It then has these experiences of immense significance. But it is a significant feature of narcotic states that they very seldom have any real objective value. And that illustrates a certain property of the conscious energy — that in itself it is not a contact with things as they really are; it is really a deeper contact with oneself that makes things matter to one in a much sharper and intense way. And so it often happens that when we have such a momentary liberation of consciousness — it happens very often in waking up, or sleep, or with the action of a narcotic, or sometimes in states of fever — we have the conviction that we see things that are of cosmic importance, truths that are ultimately real, and if by chance we write them down we find afterwards that they were nonsense, or at any rate they are something that is quite impossible to interpret. It is very important to take note of this — and this I think is confirmed by all the studies that have been made of these artificially induced conditions — because it shows why these conditions are not really a help to creative thinking, although people sometimes have hoped that they could be used for this purpose.

THE CREATIVE ENERGY

We must now return to the diagram and look at the upper-most point marked "Creative." This is the point of entry of an influence that is beyond consciousness and sensitivity. This is the creative energy which is the second cosmic energy that plays a direct part in human activity. In this lies the secret of creativity which is the subject of this lecture.

The first characteristic of the creative energy consists in the simple fact that it is beyond consciousness, or as it is more often called **supra-conscious**. It stands at the opposite pole from the automatic energy which is **subconscious**.

Unless this is understood, creativity in man must remain a mystery ascribable either to mere chance combinations or to some superhuman agency. It is a simple error of observation to suppose that creativity is conscious. I shall start then with the assertion that creativity must be ascribed to something which cannot be accounted for on the level of our conscious experience: even the intensified conscious experience that is produced by various artificial means or practices.

The second, all-important characteristic of creative energy is that, being universal, it connects us directly with the universal process. In simple language, it gives us direct access to what is really going on, whereas the other energies can give us only indirect knowledge by way of the channels of the "centres." Upon this property depends the power of **seeing** in "a new way" that is a prerequisite of creativity. A third characteristic, almost as important as that of direct contact, is the **unifying action** of the creative energy whenever it comes into play.

Before going further, I must say more about the first property of being supraconscious. We are accustomed to suppose that the more conscious an experience is, the more integration and creativity can enter into it. I am sure that anyone can verify that the creative energy does really belong to a level of activity that is supraconscious. This is by no means a new idea — it has always been held, particularly in Hindu psychology, that the condition in which man comes into contact with reality is reached only in a state of complete unconsciousness as far as the ordinary functions are concerned, the state that is called—*Turiya*. The expression "Black Light" is used in Western tradition to describe figuratively the perception which is beyond consciousness. It is a light which is not seen as light.

Sometimes people think of this fourth state of consciousness as a light so brilliant that it blinds us. For example, Plato, in the *Republic*, compares our ordinary state to people sitting in a cave chained with their backs to the entrance and looking at the shadows thrown on the wall. This corresponds, no doubt, to the screen of sensitivity that I spoke about earlier. Socrates says that if somebody were forcibly taken away from the cave and brought back into the sunlight, his eyes would pain and he would demand to be brought back into the dim light of his cave, because he could see nothing in the light of the sun. This suggests that the creative energy is no more than a higher state of consciousness to which we are not yet accustomed. This may or may not be right; but it is not very important for us at this stage, because we live on the horizontal line between sensitivity and consciousness — chiefly in the state where consciousness is absorbed into sensitivity and there is no awareness of anything but the images passing on the wall of the cave that we are looking at — that is our own sensitivity.

Now we must return to the third characteristic of creative energy, which is that it is **integrative**. Whenever it works in man, it produces an integration of his experience: things that were separate come together. Because it is supra-conscious, it appears to have the quality of spontaneity which is so striking in all creative activity.

THE IMPACT OF CREATIVE ENERGY

If we practice quietening of the mind, the first thing we notice is that the sensitive screen of the mind is crowded with a stream of thoughts — chiefly in the form of words, verbal mental associations, a kind of inner conversation — sometimes accompanied by visual images of what has been going on or is going on around us. That is the ordinary state of the sensitivity. If we succeed in quietening it, images of a different kind enter the mind. These have a higher significance, and thus enable us to understand things that we could not notice or understand at all before. That is when the consciousness has separated from the sensitivity. It is very difficult to go beyond this.

If one can come to a state of real stillness and there is a genuine problem to be solved, then the solution may appear spontaneously upon the screen of the sensitivity.

The three states can be represented by the tetradic diagram:

FIG. 10
THREE WORKINGS OF THE MIND

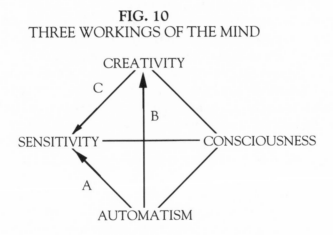

Automatic associations and images follow the first arrow, A, from the automatism to the sensitivity. The movement of understanding follows the second arrow B. The third arrow, C, represents the spontaneous creative step that cannot be explained by anything that we know or can do ourselves.

When the sensitivity has been brought to a state where it is not encumbered with the sensations and associations that arise from the automatic level — subconscious or unconscious — when it is also freed from the action of our own self-consciousness, our own personal power of understanding, then it is able to receive impressions of a quite different kind that do not seem to come from us at all, but appear to be unaccountable flashes of inspiration. The point is that they contain elements that were not in the material that we had been dealing with. They provide the missing link without which the problem could not have been solved. This explains why it is that so long as we were looking for the answer to the problem in what we already knew, there was no chance of solving it. Something had to enter that we did not and could not know.

All the great scientific discoveries have an element of this kind in them. The same, of course, is true not only of the scientific activity, but of the creative activity in art and in the affairs of life. All these originate in the Creative Energy E3 at the head of the diagram.

Now the question arises whether there are also connections to be made on the right-hand side of the diagram: for example, between the creative energy and the consciousness. Here it seems as if this is connected with **confidence** — with the conviction, even in front of an impossible situation, that there must be a way out. It may be confidence in the more ordinary sense: that which sustains us in our search for solutions to our problems, even though we can see nothing to tell us that we shall find them.

It is as if there were in us something that is already in contact with the goal toward which we are striving, and so long as we do not lose our connection with that, we shall not lose heart, we shall continue to strive. Yet another way of looking at the connection between creativity and consciousness is that it gives a certain flair, or intuition, as it is sometimes called, for what should be done in front of unusual situations. Great scientists have what people call an "uncanny" insight into the experiment that should be made in order to go forward. Whereas it would be almost impossible to arrive at the answer by plodding on, trying out all possible or all logically sensible ways of solving a problem these men cut right through and try something that would not occur to anyone else. They find what is necessary for solving the problem in a way that seems really unfair to the others who perhaps have more knowledge, better techniques, but just do not happen to have this power. I am sure that plenty of instances of this will occur to you if you study the lives of great men in every field. It seems as if that which characterizes a great man is that this particular connection is stronger than it is in ordinary people.

The lower connection on the right-hand side connecting the conscious with the automatic energies (E4 and E6) is important for understanding creativity. This connection gives the **disciplined working** that is one of the elements in all successful activity. It is said that genius is ninety-nine parts perspiration and one part inspiration. It is introduced via the connection between the consciousness and the automatism. It is this that ensures that the functional mechanisms are coordinated and directed towards what is necessary for the solution of the problem. When this connection weakens there is a constant danger of losing touch with what we are trying to achieve. Providing this connection is well-developed, many problems can be solved and unnecessary difficulties avoided. This is because the conscious energy can reveal connections upon the subconsious or automatic levels that would be missed by the sensitivity. This can also be seen, I think, in the form of skills — though I am not quite sure where one can put this. What really matters as regards this fifth connection is that there must be a certain self-directed regulation of the automatism, that we call discipline.

THE PLACE OF TRAINING IN CREATIVE ACTIVITY

Now we must turn our attention to the sixth connection between the automatic and the sensitive energies. Here also there is something to be done, but of a different kind. Our sensitivity is not given once and for all, in the way that a cinematograph screen is given so that all we have to do is vary the images that are thrown on it, but not the response of the screen itself. Our sensitivity is much more highly organized than a "screen." It is sometimes said that the sensitivity is a "clean slate on which nature writes" — as I think William James called it. The modern view, due to students of child psychology such as Piaget, inclines to the belief that the sensitivity cooperates actively in the formation of mental images. The development of the automatic mechanisms is not really analogous to "dirtying the clean slate." In fact, our sensitivity is like a **body within the body**. That is why this sensitivity has sometimes even been called the second body; some people call it the astral body. Gurdjieff names it the *Kesdjan body*, to indicate that it can have an organization of its own so complete that it can lead an independent existence. I am sure that there is much truth in this view that the sensitivity itself can be organized to become an independent body, but that is hard to demonstrate. It is quite easy to demonstrate that our sensitivity is capable of being trained and organized, and that our effectiveness in any kind of work that we have to do is very much influenced by the degree of organization and receptiveness of the sensitive energy. It is quite a different sort of training from the training that is suitable for developing the automatic functions. We can train each of the centres — instinctive, moving, emotional, and mental — by repetition, by pressure of attention, by suffering, and so on. In this way, the automatism acquires various skills. All this belongs to the same category as Pavlov's conditioning of reflexes. Here we have something quite different. If the sensitivity is to be trained, it has to accept guidance by the consciousness; because, until the consciousness can stand away from it in order to do something with it, then the sensitivity keeps its habitual yes-no, like-dislike reactions. The training of sensitivity is not attained by conditioning, it is attained by the very reverse: by **de-conditioning**, by setting it free from all the habitual reactions that come from the automatism.

This is very important for understanding all processes of training and learning. If we fail to keep these different parts of the human totality clearly separated in our dealings both with children and with ourselves in our own training, we can produce quite lamentable results. For example, we can condition the sensitivity so that it becomes almost incapable of receiving new impressions or responding to new ideas spontaneously. This means not only loss of creativity, but even loss of our own consciousness; whereas, what is required is that all conditioning and training should be **transferred directly to the automatism**. The automatic energy cannot work in any other way, and it requires to be conditioned, but it must be conditioned in such a way that the sensitivity is not conditioned at the same time. It is quite possible to bring our sensitivity towards the state of non-conditioning, while at the same time not sacrificing all the skills and powers that come from a well-conditioned, well-trained automatism.

✛

QUESTIONS

Q. Is luck a means of producing conscious energy? Or is luck an illusion, or is it produced perhaps by the creative energy?
J.G.B. Things may appear like luck, because we do not know how they come about: but there is also real luck and this does come from the creative energy.

Q. When one intentionally produces a visual image is it conscious energy working through sensitivity?
J.G.B. Yes, visualizing is the projection of images on the sensitivity from the consciousness, instead of from the automatism. We must not confuse conscious "imagining" with the automatic

unintentional appearance of images which constantly emerge from the automatism into the sensitivity. If you say: "I will see a lemon suspended in mid-air there in front of me," and you not only see the lemon; but your mouth begins to feel the taste of lemon, then that is probably produced by a projection of the conscious energy on to the sensitive screen. The experience, the taste of bitterness of the lemon, and the shape and colour of it all are actually experienced in the sensitive energy. We call such experiences "imagination," but they are really only sensitivity.

Q. When images come from the automatic energy, in the case of a lemon, is it somehow like a memory?
J.G.B. Yes. Nothing will come from the automatism that has not previously come into it from the senses. I think it is probably true to say that if we are going to produce an image like that of a lemon, we have to make use of the memories already available in the automatism.

Q. Is there not one property of this sensitive part which is something like the following: that if there is some new insight, then it seems that this side of it tends to produce very rapid proliferation of things around it, which happens extremely quickly; that if one consciously can see a new connection, then very rapidly this connection is transferred to a number of other related domains. There is a danger that this becomes out of hand because it has this expansive quality. Have you found that?
J.G.B. It is quite true. This comes because of the lack of the power to hold sensitivity and consciousness apart. This is connected with the **inner strength** of the person concerned. A weak man can have such flashes, but they will collapse on to the sensitive energy and will be simply experienced. The result may be excitement and interest and, as you say, proliferation and images; but there is something lacking, and that is the withdrawn consciousness which is able to make judgements as to **what shall be accepted as understanding**. Your having said that reminds me that I did not

refer to one of the most important properties of conscious energy, and that is the power of judgement associated with it.

Q. I would like to ask a question about separation on the horizontal plane. I have found that in moments of really getting to see something, there appears to come a very strong force which acts against the separation and attracts them together — it is difficult to bear.

J.G.B. This is a very true and very important observation. There is a very strong polarity between the sensitive and the conscious energies; they are like male and female powers and they attract one another very strongly. This is really our difficulty; if we try to what is called "remember ourselves," which means to keep separate the consciousness and the sensitivity, we see that as soon as we take our eyes off them, at once they go into a guilty embrace!

One way of studying this distinction between sensitivity and consciousness is the practice of trying to stop thoughts; that is, trying to empty the mind of thoughts. That, by itself, requires that you should have this separation, and with this, first of all you see this tremendous pull that there is which draws us back. The single-valued awareness of what is going on is usual; but how difficult it is to be **conscious of being aware** of what is going on. And yet, this being conscious of being aware of what is going on can arise spontaneously, involuntarily, with no action on our own part. To maintain this intentionally is very difficult. But even to do this for a few moments from time to time, will help you to see that you can produce in yourself voluntarily two distinct levels in your conscious experience; one is the level of **sensitivity**, and the other the level of **consciousness**. I will quote a verse out of the *Rig Veda* which shows how ancient the idea of separating sensitivity and consciousness is.

> *Two birds, fast-yoked companions*
> *Both clasp the self-same tree.*
> *One eats the sweet fruit and*
> *The other looks on without eating.*

The two birds are sensitivity and consciousness, and they are fast-yoked in us. But it does not mean that they cannot be kept apart from one another, because unquestionably they can. It is also possible to suppress the sensitivity and produce a state that we call **unconscious**. For example, states of anesthesia, when there is no reaction to sense stimulation, can be produced in various ways and yet the consciousness remains. Everyone who has been in a deep coma and has memories of it knows his peculiar thing, that one can have suppression of the **sensitivity** and simultaneous liberation of **consciousness**. That is an extreme case, but there is any amount of evidence that these two are really distinct from one another. is most important characteristic of our nature is seldom taken into account. When we become aware of its immense significance, it is like awakening from a hypnotic sleep. This awakening is the first step towards the fulfillment of our destiny as men.

✛

LECTURE V

The Last Question

I N THIS LAST LECTURE, I am going to venture into regions where
we have little to guide us, except analogy and confidence in the
rule that every part must bear some imprint of the whole to which
it belongs. The energies that we can discover in our experience
and the ways in which they are transformed and used are pointers
to the higher energies that are beyond any direct human perception. We can hope to reach, in thought at least, the limits of the
Natural World — beyond those limits is the mystery of the Source
and Origin of all that exists. Even if this mystery were revealed to
us — and perhaps it is revealed within Creation here and everywhere — we could not understand it, for we are natural, limited
beings. The Infinite and the truly Supernatural are set apart by a
difference of kind, not of scale or even content. The Infinite and
the Supernatural are "here and now," but this makes it no easier for
us to recognize them.

One great advantage of the approach we have followed in
these lectures is that we have been able to connect everything with
one definite aspect of our experience — the "power of doing
work," to which we have given the name of "Energy." So defined,
Energy is ubiquitous, for all experience is in action, and it is also of
action. We can go to the limit and think of a Supreme Energy by
which the entire universe is created and sustained. This is what I
have called the Transcendent Energy; but I must remind you that

91

even this hypothetical Prime Source Energy is still within the bounds of Creation. We are not to think of it as God, though it may well be the highest and purest instrument of the Divine Will. Energies are only **powers** which have to be exercised. This requires, first, the **will** to exercise them, and second, the **being** in and through which they are to act. In other words, the study of energy cannot tell us all that we want to know about Man, Creation, and God. It does not tell us what anything or anyone **is**; nor does it tell us the purpose that energy transformations are to serve. It can, however, tell us how this purpose is being accomplished in the world and so help us to understand what we learn in other ways about Being and Will.

It is probably true to say that the entire universe with its myriads of galaxies is a vast apparatus for the transformation of energy. The solar system, and with it our earth, is a very small apparatus in comparison with one galaxy; but it is huge compared with individual man. We men are enormous compared with atoms. Some of the most astonishing discoveries of the present century concern the unimaginable differences in scale as we pass from one level of existence to another. Throughout the whole range, the transformations of energy are a connecting link and a means of understanding. For example, almost all that we know about the universe outside our solar system concerns transformations of energy. The modern science of astrophysics is wholly based upon study of transformations of energies in stars and galaxies. It is only on the scale of our own existence that we can hope to learn about Being and Will; on all other scales, we can observe only the manifestations produced by energy transformations.

In the domain of human experience, our subjective observation of what is happening is mainly confined to the range from sensitivity to consciousness. This is what we call the "mind" or "awareness." Outside this narrow band of energies, we can observe little beyond the results of transformations. This is the principal reason for the division of "mind" and "matter" which was regarded by many philosophers since Descartes as absolute. The recognition of the "relativity of materiality" breaks this division down; but it leaves the distinction of conscious and unconscious mental processes to be accounted for. In Lecture III, I made a brief reference to the four-fold division of automatic, sensitive, conscious, and creative sources of our experience. This division is only relative, for the automatic passes over into the vital processes and these in turn into the biochemical transformations of energy at the threshold of life. Thus, the "subconscious" has its foundation in the truly unconscious regions where life emerges from inert states of matter. This is also an upward transition that leads from consciousness to creativity and from creativity to the Universal Cosmic Energies that I have called Unitive and Transcendent. These connect us with the mystery of the operation of the Supreme Will within the Created World. We cannot conceive the possibility of going beyond Creation to seek an answer to the question: "Why has the World been created?" We can, however, go some way toward answering the secondary question: "If there need be a world at all, why such a world as we see about us?" This question can, at least partly, be answered in terms of what Gurdjieff called the *Laws of World Creation and World Maintenance*, saying that one of the obligatory strivings of every being endowed with reason is to understand these laws better.

In saying that we can go some way toward answering ultimate questions, I do not want to suggest that no mystery will remain. A fair definition of "mystery" can be given by saying that all that is beyond consciousness belongs to the realm of mystery. Accordingly, the operations of the three highest cosmic energies — creative, unitive, and transcendent — must be mysterious except as they enter conscious experience. Since our human consciousness can apprehend only a very small part of these operations, the element of mystery must always predominate. Even this is not the end of mystery. Consciousness itself is mysterious because it cannot describe itself. Consciousness can stand aside from sensation, automatism, and the working of all the lower energies and by standing back can observe, modify and, to some extent, control them. But consciousness cannot observe, modify, and control itself. This is the key to understanding the problem of human transformation: the necessary modifications in the structure of our consciousness can be brought about only through the operations of the higher energy of creativity. These operations are not capricious or arbitrary, but conform to their own laws. These laws in turn derive from the Universal Energies E2 and E1. We can reach some understanding of these higher operations, by invoking the principle of universal similarity which amounts to the expectation that what we know can give us some clue to what we do not know. We shall do our best to see how the "Laws of World Creation and World Maintenance" can be detected in human experience and so transferred to the mysterious realm that is beyond the reach of our consciousness.

THE PENTADS

In the second volume of *The Dramatic Universe* (Chapter 35), I have shown how Gurdjieff's *Table of All Life* can be understood with the help of the five-term system or Pentad. The progression of systems described in the Introduction to Volume II introduces into the worlds of our experience a sequence of attributes comprising: universality (the monad), complementarity (the dyad), relatedness (the triad), activity (the tetrad), and potentiality or significance (the pentad). So, if we want to answer the question: "What is the significance of human life in the scheme of things?" — we should look to a five-term system for our answer. The significance of any being, class of beings, situation, historical event — or indeed anything of which one can ask the question, "What is the meaning and purpose of this?" — has three distinct aspects. The first aspect is its significance in and for itself: this can be called **intrinsic**. The second is measured by its potentialities which span all the levels with which the particular entity is in direct contact.

FIG. 11a
THE FIVE LEVELS OF HUMAN
SIGNIFICANCE

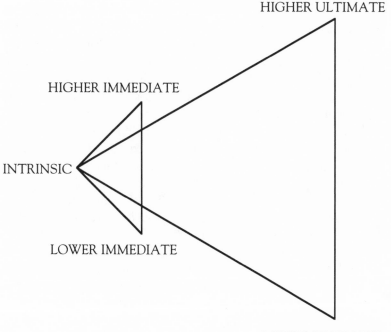

Because of this property of direct contact, we call the second aspect of significance **immediate**. The third aspect is given by the extreme limits of its possible participation in the world process. This is called **ultimate**.

Since significance is obviously connected with such notions as "place occupied," "level of being," "potentiality for influencing processes" — both immediate and ultimate significance have higher and lower limits. This is how we arrive at the five terms of the pentad.

We can take, as an example, man whose life is centred in his sensitivity (E5). Since sensitivity is the highest life energy, we can say that man centred in sensitivity enjoys the fullness of life. This enjoyment is the intrinsic significance of his existence. His field of action ranges from automatism to consciousness. All psychic functions operating on the level of automatic energy (E6) are at his disposal. He is also able to reach the state of self-consciousness (E4) which is the highest level at which he is able to function. Nevertheless, he cannot be said to be self-sufficient, for he cannot control his own consciousness, nor can he exercise his powers except in the environment of his earthly life which includes the human society. In Jungian language, he can find the meaning of his life only in the Collective Unconscious which is the source of creativity upon his own scale. The upper limit of his significance is E3, representing the total potentiality of human nature. The lower limit of his significance derives from his participation in the universal life process or the vital energy E7.

All this can be represented diagrammatically in the pentad symbol I introduced in *The Dramatic Universe* (Chapter 35), though I now prefer a somewhat modified shape for the figure. The intrinsic significance is placed on the left and the ultimate significance on the right with the immediate significance between them.

When we use this to represent the aspect of significance of sensitive or "animal" man, we have the symbol of Figure 11.

The vertical lines represent the range of the inner and outer significance of "sensitive" man. The radial lines show the connections between the activity of his "mind" (E5) and the various domains in which he can find fulfillment. There is an immense wealth of meaning in this simple diagram. I advise you to take each

FIG. 11
THE SIGNIFICANCE OF SENSITIVITY

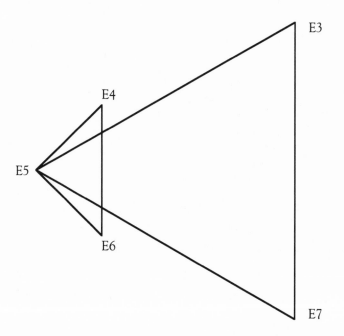

of the ten lines connecting every pair of points and ask yourselves
how you would interpret their significance.

FIG. 12
THE TEN MODES OF SIGNIFICANCE

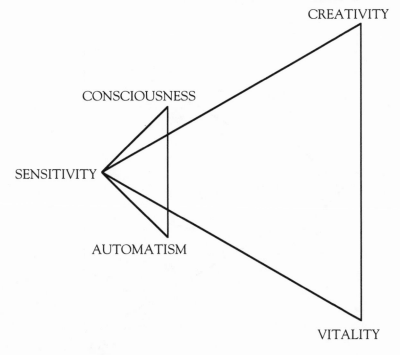

To give you an idea of the way to set about it, I will say
something about the connection between Creativity (E3) and
Vitality (E7). Life is the field of the unceasing creative activity by
which the Universe is in process of realizing the purpose of its
existence. The vital energy is the lowest or "coarsest" in which

there are the rudiments of free choice. Vital energy can do no more than accept or reject what is presented to it; but this is an immense advance on the deterministic working of the construc-tive energy which cannot depart from the predetermined patterns of life. Creativity within Creation (as distinct from the Creation of Creation) is possible only where there is some freedom of response. The entire range of creative activity lies between E7 and E3. Conversely, the upper limit of life is the creation of life itself and this according to Gurdjieff is an independent creation within the creation, the source of which is the creative power of the sun and the stars. All of this and very much more can be discovered from an attentive consideration of the vertical line from Vitality to Creativity in Figure 12. Equally significant interpretation can be found for each of the other nine connecting lines. For those of you who are familiar with Ouspensky's scheme of "Seven Levels of Man" (*In Search of the Miraculous*[4]), I would say that "Sensitive" man comprises all the first four: Man No. 1, No. 2, No. 3, and No. 4. Only Man No. 4 is sensitive in all his centres. The remainder are sensitive in one centre and automatic in the others.

THE PENTAD OF CONSCIOUSNESS

All that I have been saying applies to men whose interest in life is centred in their own sensitivity. This means all the experi-ences that are presented to them through the senses and the psychic centres of thought, feeling, movement, and sex. We must now see what happens to a man when his significance is trans-ferred from sensitivity to consciousness. One way to describe this is to call it the transition from dream life to waking life. Experi-ence associated with no energy higher than sensitive is dependent upon images projected on the sensitivity. It cannot give direct contact either with ourselves or with any other object. This is what is meant by the statement that the life of sensitive or animal man is a dream state. There is certainly a great change when the whole organism is sensitized to produce what Ouspensky calls Man No. 4. Unlike most people, such a man is awake in all his functions and his automatic processes occupy their right place as instruments of the will. When this is achieved, the separation of sensitivity and consciousness becomes easy and the state of self-remembering arises whenever it is needed. Nevertheless, there is no complete and permanent change of nature until there is a transition of the Will from sensitivity to consciousness. For this, we have to pass over the gap that divides life processes from cosmic processes. Until the will is transferred across the gap, the tendency to revert to the sleeping state remains.

There is a powerful attraction between consciousness and sensitivity that resembles the attraction between the sexes and indeed has the same origin in the mutual need that draws the vital

FIG. 13
CREATIVITY AND CONSCIOUSNESS

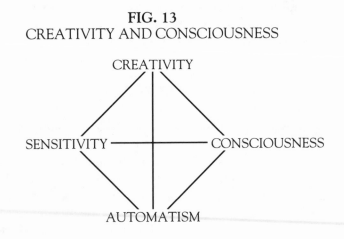

and cosmic energies to produce the material world. When this attraction is overcome, the creative energy is brought into play. We then have the "complete" man, represented by the tetrad with the cross as its symbol.

The situation represented by this symbol has several features that are surprising from the standpoint of our usual modes of thought.

The separation of sensitivity and consciousness is possible only if life is not an end in itself. This can be seen if we turn the symbol round so that the life energies are on one level and the cosmic on another.

FIG.14
THE LIFE LIMIT

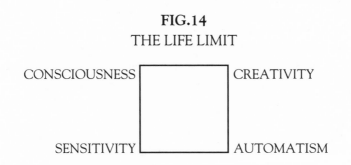

CONSCIOUSNESS   CREATIVITY

SENSITIVITY   AUTOMATISM

This figure conveys the notion of life as an upper limit of one mode of existence and conscious creativity as the lower limit of another mode of existence. It evokes for us the picture of "two worlds." One of these "exists" in the usual sense of the word as that which we know through the senses and the mind (sensitivity E5) and is acted upon through the automatic mechanisms of our body and the instruments it can make. The "other" world is beyond life, beyond mind (sensitivity), and is reached through consciousness.

Man cannot act upon the world of consciousness, but he can participate in it through creative activity. This world **is** by virtue of unceasing *creation*. It is not material in the ordinary sense and yet it is a world of energies and it depends upon energy transformations just as much as the world of sense experience.

Man links the two worlds together. This is one of the principal reasons for his existence and his significance depends upon his ability to play his role. The "sensitive" man I described a few minutes ago links consciousness and sensitivity by reducing all to the level of sensitivity, or as we ordinarily call it, **mind**. The "conscious" man can separate himself from his own mind and so make a creative bridge between sensation and creativity, between Life and the Cosmos. Ouspensky distinguishes three levels of conscious man. All three are beyond the limitations of terrestrial existence, but they differ profoundly in the location of their Will. Man No. 5 has his centre of gravity in consciousness (E4). Man No. 6 is in creativity (E3). Man no. 7 has reached the limit of human perfection and is merged into the Unitive Energy (E2). I shall come later to this supreme achievement of human self-realization.

The whole scheme can be represented by the pentad symbol shown on page 103.

The interpretation of this symbol is fairly straightforward, until we come to the ultimate upper limit which corresponds to Man No. 7, whose significance I shall speak of later. The first point is to notice that the intrinsic or central significance of Man No. 5 is consciousness itself. Consciousness of Self — the Man with his own Permanent "I" — the Man of the Soul — the Man who has found himself in himself: all these and many other descriptions are given to the man whose significance is centred in consciousness. He can find within himself, as the upper limit of his own nature, the power of creativity. He is the master of his own sensitivity, the ruler of his mind and of all its attendant powers. He maintains his existence by drawing upon his automatism. Herein lies a most important difference from sensitive man who exists at

FIG. 15
THE SIGNIFICANCE OF CONSCIOUS MAN

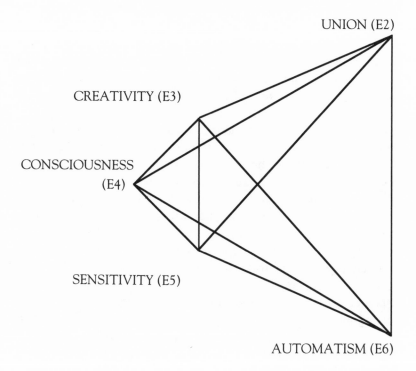

the expense of life and is therefore mortal. Conscious man exists at the expense of his own automatism and is therefore beyond the reach of the vital processes (E7) of organic life and death.

The powers of conscious man do not exhaust the potentialities latent in human nature. Man No. 5 lacks the free creative power which comes from the ability to pass through the barrier of consciousness into the strange world where creativity is the only reality and where things are only what they are made to be. The man who has established himself in that world has powers in the ordinary world that ordinary people cannot understand. He is called Man No. 6. Beyond that again is the man established in Unity. His relationship to creativity is the same as that of sensitive man to automatism. Whatever level a man's will has reached, he is able to treat the content of the lower levels as instruments to be used.

These ideas are very hard to grasp until you have begun to understand the difference between two opposite ways of existing. Gurdjieff calls these the *Itoklanoz* and the *Fulasnitamnian principles*. The first corresponds to man of the first four kinds who depends upon external stimulation for all that he does. The second is the way of conscious men who receive their energy from the Cosmic Tetrad. Conscious man is in varying degrees an independent Will and he can create for himself whatever vehicle he may need for his work. You will realize that the division into two is an oversimplification. As we have just seen, there are distinct gradations or orders of Conscious Man, but all have in common the immensely significant property of having access to Sources of energy that are beyond life. This is not easy to understand, for we are accustomed to see people of the first three kinds whose supply of energy depends upon the state of their organism. Those who can draw upon Creative Energy (E3) have power over their bodily organism and over all their life functions including the transformations of sensitive energy (E5). They are also totally different from ordinary people in the manner of their death. The ordinary man who lives in his sensitive energy has contact with the objective world only through sensation and thought, both of which are functions of the physical organism. When he dies, his sensitive energy continues to experience, but the experience is that of the dream state. With the majority of people, the dream state appears as a continuation of life, so that they cannot realize that they are "dead." This realization depends upon consciousness, which is usually absorbed into sensitivity and so loses the power to "see things as they are."

The dream state may persist — it is said that first the consequences of wrong actions are suffered and afterwards the rewards of good actions are experienced as a state of timeless bliss that is called "Paradise." Only those whose will is fixed upon the attainment of Reality break through the dream state and experience the definitive separation of consciousness from sensitivity that is called by Gurdjieff the *Second Sacred Rascooarno* or the *Second and Final Death*. Those who have passed over the gap that separates life from cosmic existence are liberated from the limitations of existence and can create for themselves whatever form they need.

The descriptions I have just given are based upon traditional beliefs: but they agree with the conclusions I have drawn from the study of energies.

I have spoken of the mystery of death, not to claim that I am able to reveal its secrets, but to show you that from a knowledge of energies and their characteristics we can construct a picture that does not conflict either with everyday experience or with religious beliefs. Such a picture has more than theoretical value, for it can help us to see what is required if we are to be free from bondage to the influences not only of the material world, but of the worlds of life also. There is a strange paradox in the transition from sensitivity to consciousness. The sensitive man has the illusion of self. This is due to the absorption of conscious energy into the sensitivity. The conscious man is in the process of forming a vehicle or "body" that is independent of the processes of life. This vehicle is sometimes called the "soul" or the "Higher Being Body." Even when it is incomplete, it allows the consciousness to exercise an independent "Will" and this is the beginning of a "True Self" or "I". Nevertheless, conscious Man No. 5 does not have the illusion of selfhood, for he is aware that his consciousness depends upon the Creative Energy (E3) that he cannot control. The paradox lies in the reality of individual or personal freedom and the absence of any sense of selfhood or personal identity. You may see the point of the paradox if I remind you of the aphorism: "Freedom is to be free from the illusion that one is free, doing comes from the realization of non-doing." The resolution of the paradox lies in understanding that Creativity is beyond Consciousness. The conscious man, by virtue of the Creative Energy which has become part of his own nature, is free and able to "do"; but he is not "conscious" of the Source of his own freedom and power. He can draw from the Source and he is, at all times, sustained and renewed by his contact with it; but he is not in it and cannot know it, much less command it!

There is another most important characteristic of the first level of conscious man to which I must refer before going further. This is his ability to separate himself from his instruments. Sensitive man is constantly in danger of identifying himself with his sensations, feelings, thoughts, and especially with sensitivity itself — that is, with his "Mind." Conscious man is aware of all these as instruments and he never makes the mistake of regarding his "Mind" as "himself," any more than he could regard the mirror in which he sees his body as being the body itself. Sensitivity has been called the "mirror of experience" and the images thrown on the mirror are the "contents of the mind." Sensitive men, especially those who are partly automatic, cannot verify this state of affairs, for their experience is almost wholly restricted to their "mind." The onset of consciousness alters the picture inasmuch as "self-observation" in the true sense of "self-observing self" begins to be possible. It is not until full self-consciousness is established that the "externalization of the mind" is complete.

In a sense, the inability of sensitive men to apprehend the true state of affairs is a merciful necessity. It preserves them from remembering their own mortality and from realizing their state of delusion, and so enables them to deal with the affairs of life competently, even if not creatively.

Creativity is indeed a two-edged sword. In the presence of creativity, life itself is humbled. For one whose very being is centred in the processes of life, creativity is terrifying. To create, one must "die" — that is, one must give up this illusion of doing. At the moment when mind abdicates, creativity is enthroned. The surrender of mind may come by exhaustion of effort, by an accidental withdrawal of attention, by a powerful shock or stimulus, by various ascetic practices, or by a conscious act of will. There are some rare men who, without transformation of nature, have a natural gift of "stilling the mind," and in them creativity may be active without a corresponding realization of their own nothingness. Such men are dangerous for themselves and others; but they also fulfill a role that has to be played inasmuch as they are channels for the introduction of creative impulses that give new directions to the life process that flows between the constructive and sensitive energies with new power to change itself.

I think I ought to stop here for a moment to say that there are conditions of human existence below the level of sensitivity. Even Man No. 1, who is sensitive in his body, but automatic in thought and feeling, is not the "lowest grade" man. There are men who are almost wholly automatic, who have little sensitivity in any of their functions; and there are, of course, sub-normal or "defective" people who scarcely rise above the level of the vital or vegetative energy. These people are also necessary for the processes of transformation and we should feel great sympathy toward them. Their chances depend entirely upon others; that is perhaps why they so often attract intense parental devotion. They can be the means of developing consciousness and even creativity in others and they share in the benefits of this development.

THE HIGHEST HUMAN MYSTERY

Now we must leave the subject of Consciousness and Creativity and turn our attention again to the Pentad of Conscious

Man and examine the highest point which is occupied by the Unitive Energy E2. This tells us that man finds his fulfillment or completion in the second highest energy of the twelve-term series. I have not yet said much about the two highest energies, partly because we can, in any case, know them only in a very narrow and limited way, and partly because I have intended to say all that I could in this last lecture. There is a third reason for caution and that is that once we pass the truth level, we touch the hem of Deity. If the word Transcendent means anything, it must refer to that which is beyond existence and hence uncreated. Such notions belong to theology and not the study of energies. Therefore, when I speak of the two highest energies, you must understand that I do so **as they appear to us**, not as they are in their own nature.

The greatest unitive force we know is love, and it is generally agreed that love must also be a Cosmic Power enveloping and reconciling all that exists. When we say that God is Love, we may mean this or we may mean more than we can hope to understand. There are two ways of approaching an understanding of the two highest energies. The first is to extrapolate from below, making use of what we can discover about the lower energies and of the assumption or hypothesis that if there are four gradations of the material energies and four of the life energies, there should also be four cosmic energies. Combining this assumption with the notion of an ultimate total state in which all processes have their origin, we get the idea of Transcendent Energy. Taking this idea together with that of consciousness, we form the notion of an energy that is both universal and also intimately present in all experience. This energy must serve as a link between the Transcendent Energy by which the entire cosmos is sustained and the Creative Energy that directs the detailed working out of the Cosmic Purpose. This implies a mission of adaptation and even of reconciliation that we can, without forcing the interpretation, designate as a mission of love. The second approach is to start from the problem of accounting for the world as we meet it in our ordinary awareness. It is a world of suffering, injustice, and unresolved conflicts. Nature, red in tooth and claw; humanity, steeped in cruelty and egoism; and all the intimate failures of our personal lives, confront us in stark opposition to the deep conviction shared by almost everyone that somewhere and somehow there is a way out and that what appears meaningless on one level must make sense upon another. As we cannot find that "other world" in any conscious experience, we place it beyond the limits of human consciousness. Once we begin to grasp the significance of creativity, we can see that it cannot be associated with the qualities of Love and Unity. Creativity disturbs in order to enrich. Love impoverishes in order to unite. Creativity is the enrichment of consciousness. Love restores the unity that creativity by its very nature perpetually disrupts. By such arguments we arrive at the conclusion that there must be a power beyond creativity with the corollary that this Power must be able to penetrate into our lives directly but into our experience only indirectly.

We should not be surprised at the conclusion that we can have no direct experience of the Unitive Energy. We have seen that consciousness itself is already left behind by the Creative Energy. If Unitive Energy has the quality of love, then there is nothing to prevent us from saying that Love is everywhere but we cannot be conscious of it; nor even experience its action upon our consciousness as we can with the Creative Energy. This may seem to you to be a most unsatisfying conclusion. In our human experience, we believe that we know what love is and we even believe that we are able to "love"; that is, to produce intentionally in ourselves the operations of the Unitive Energy. We may have a modest opinion of our own capacity for loving; but we seldom question that men have loved with the fullness of love. We may be uncertain as to the absolute status of sexual love, and yet believe that human love can rise to such heights as to give us a picture of what the Universal Love may really be.

The scheme that we have been working out in these lectures suggests a very different conclusion. Since the experience of love actually occurs, and since it can be associated with all human functions and powers, we may assume that the Unitive Energy can manifest at all levels of existence. I shall come later to the cosmic significance of this assumption; for the time being, let us look at it in human terms only. Let us take the whole range of energies associated with human experience, starting from vital energy E7. Love at this level is organic affinity without awareness of what is happening. At the next stage, we have automatic love E6. This is experienced as natural attraction unconnected with "mind." The love that we are commonly aware of is on the sensitive level (E5). Love of Consciousness is totally different, because it is participation in the tetrad of Cosmic Energies. It is Universal and at the same time Individual. Through Love of Consciousness man finds himself in another and another in himself. Those of you who are familiar with Gurdjieff's *All and Everything* will recall the marble tablet of Ashiata Shiemash, with the inscription:

> *Love of consciousness evokes the same in response.*
> *Love of feeling evokes the opposite.*
> *Love of body depends only on type and polarity.*

This aphorism conveys the distinctions between the Unitive Energy associated respectively with Consciousness, Sensitive, and Automatic states.

So far, the progression is not hard to follow. The question next comes as to whether man can experience Creative Love (E3). The answer is certainly quite different for sensitive and for conscious man. The former cannot experience Creative Love — it is the upper limit of his pentad — but he can be "received into it." This may suggest to you the idea of "Paradise" or the state of blessedness that is attainable by right discipline of the sensitivity. Creative Love holds a very different significance for Conscious Man. It is beyond his consciousness, but for him it is "second nature." The process of transformation to which he submits himself engenders in him the *Impartial and Objective Love* that Gurdjieff regards as one of the highest manifestations possible for a three-brained being. Through Creative Love, conscious man willingly accepts the burden of existence, which means participation in all the joys and sufferings of the world. But whereas for the world, joy and suffering are opposing, even contradictory states, conscious man unites them in his experience, neither cleaving to the one nor seeking to escape the other. By his impartial and objective attitude towards all beings, he becomes a factor of union and reconciliation. In this way he is an instrument of Cosmic Love within the limitations of his own Individuality.

I must refer you to *The Dramatic Universe*, Volume II, Chapters 27-30, for an explanation of Individuality and for an account of the various gradations of Individuality that are possible for man. Some men become conscious, but on a small scale and their task is correspondingly restricted. Others may be the vehicles of an Individuality that is Universal and they can pass beyond consciousness into the realm of Creative Energy (E3) or even can attain to the Unitive Energy whereby they become one with Cosmic Love and Wisdom. Embracing all existence is the Transcendent Energy E1 that is beyond the reach of any finite being. If you reflect upon the hints I have given you, you will see that they will throw light upon almost all the problems of man and his destiny and even help you to understand the mysteries of religion. But you must not forget what I said earlier: that none of the four Cosmic Energies are directly knowable in sensitive experience. We can think about them, feel about them, search for them and respond to them only as they are transmitted into the world in which we live. So long as we remain on the sensitive level, we shall have divided and contradictory experience. If we fall below that to the automatic level, we are no more than "man machines," cut off from any contact with cosmic realities. If we can raise ourselves beyond life to consciousness, then and then only will these Realities become real for us. This will explain the subtitle of the last of Gurdjieff's writings, *Life is Real only then when I AM*. [5]

THE FINAL QUESTION

If *I* AM is the key to Reality, we have still to face the question: What is this Reality? If we could answer this final question, all our problems would be resolved. Contrary to what seems to be taught in many ancient traditions, I do not believe that we men can ever come near to the answer. It is claimed that man can achieve the "Beatific Vision" or God-Realization, in which Reality is known face to face. Those who claim to have had this vision confess that they cannot describe it nor produce any evidence — valid for others than themselves — that it is not illusion or subjective ecstasy. We may believe that there is a path that leads from mind to consciousness, from consciousness through the "black night" to creativity, and from this, by the cessation of all activity, to the unitive state in which man is totally transformed. But this does not mean that he has reached Ultimate Reality. He has come to the utmost limit of participation in Reality that is possible for a finite being — but the Infinite must remain forever inaccessible. Nevertheless, the experience, *if authentic*, is evidence that man can go far, far beyond any conscious experience that can be understood with the mind. But how are we to know that it is authentic? The difficulty is not only that those who claim to have attained it cannot account for or even describe what has happened to them. We have to take into account the well-known fact that the conviction of having seen Reality "face to face" can be reached in various ways. It is common enough in a certain type of insanity. It can be induced artificially by drugs and various ascetic practices or even by accidental shocks. The explanation is not hard to find in the light of our study of energies. The sense of direct perception of ultimate reality is nothing more than the result of an influx of creative energy (E3) into a mind that has been emptied of its usual contents by one of the various actions: mental illness, drugs, shock, etc. As evidence of "Reality" the experience is valueless, except insofar as valid, important and quite new ideas or images are presented to the mind. Even so, they are not the same as the influx of Unitive Energy. This influx does not produce any kind of verifiable result, nor does it produce ecstatic or other wonderful experiences. It enters and withdraws again, leaving behind a nature profoundly transformed but no direct perception of Reality.

I have studied many descriptions of these states and have met and talked with men who have achieved them. To some extent, I can even say that I know them by personal experience. They are sometimes very real and very important, but they are not Revelations of Ultimate Reality or Truth.

Can we then have any idea of what Reality means? To this, I would reply that even if we can never see Reality in its infinite totality, we can know it *in one of its aspects*. Reality is not only infinitely great, it is also infinitely diverse in its **qualities**. This is a greater barrier to our perception than infinite magnitude. Our powers of perceiving through the senses and of forming mental images are very limited and there is no doubt that, for this reason alone, there are elements of Reality right in front of us that we do not suspect. Some of these come to light indirectly — as for example, we have discovered the tremendous source of energy within atoms. This has been in front of man and was almost made evident when Becquerel and Curie discovered the radioactive elements. And yet it was not recognized for more than fifty years. Some discoveries such as that of magnetism or of micro-organisms have come after mankind has been familiar with their indirect effects for thousands of years. So, we may expect that new aspects of Nature, at present unsuspected, will become known in the future. But it is also almost certain that much will remain forever inaccessible to man for lack of any possible means of knowing it.

It does not follow from this that broad, general ideas about the nature of Reality can have no validity. Whenever we observe some aspect of Nature that is invariably present in all phenomena on all scales, we are justified in regarding it as a clue to the nature of the Whole. The transformation of energies is *just such an aspect*.

Time is another aspect of nature that we meet with everywhere and a little reflection will show that time and the transformations of energy are inseparable. Eddington was one of the first to point out that irreversible transformations of energy are the only signposts we know that "point the direction of time."

Let us see what all this means to us men. We are involved in the universal transformations of energy and we are involved in a very special way because of our situation astride the life energies and the cosmic energies. We have the power to choose between sensitivity (E5) and consciousness (E4). When we look at this closely, we can see that it means choosing between the **irreversible** time of the life process and the **reversible** or free time of the cosmic process. This idea may surprise you, unless you are familiar with the cosmic energies. This unique situation involves us men in a special responsibility for our own energy transformations. I spoke earlier about the distinction between man centred in sensitivity (E5), that is, the **lower mind**, and man centred in consciousness (E4) that is, the **higher mind**. We have the power to choose between these two transformations. When we look at it closely, we can see that it is equivalent to choosing between the limited and irreversible processes of life that end in death and the unlimited and open processes of the self-realization of the entire existing world that probably have no end.

Man is an apparatus for the transformation of energies; but he is a very peculiar kind of apparatus that has **the power to choose how it shall be used**. We can be used by Nature for its own purpose or we can be used by the Supernatural Power for a supernatural purpose. This choice is put before man by all religions; but it is not easy to see what it means objectively. With the help of some knowledge of energies, we can give a very precise meaning to the choice.

We can go one step further, and look at the means whereby the choice is made possible. It is because we are penetrated by the Unitive Energy E2, which is beyond our own nature and yet is able to connect us with the highest energy of all: the Transcendent Energy by which the entire existing world is sustained and directed.

It is tempting to interpret these conclusions in philosophical or religious terms. You can see for yourselves how this could be done. The Unitive Energy can be called Divine Love; the Transcendent Energy can be called the Spirit of God by which the world is created. Creative Energy can be associated with the Angelic Powers. Consciousness can be called conscience or even the Guardian Angel. But I must warn you that such attempts at transferring the results of studying one aspect of Reality and applying them to a different aspect are almost certain to be misleading. We have no grounds whatever — except the desire to find analogies — for drawing any conclusions outside the field of energy transformations. Within this field, we can go as far as the line of thought we have followed will permit. The most significant conclusion is that in this aspect, man is a cosmic apparatus for the transformation of energies and his destiny depends upon the way he chooses to perform his task. This is the answer to the final question regarding energies. There is a great Cosmic Purpose to be served and we men have the ability to serve it and also the freedom to choose how and even if we shall serve it. The very nature of our service is that it must be freely given or it is useless. By giving it, we enter the path of infinite fulfillment; by refusing it we enter the path of dream life that ends in nothingness.

4P. D. Ouspensky, *In Search of the Miraculous*, Harcourt Brace Jovanovich (Orlando, Florida: 1977).
5G. I. Gurdjieff, *Life is real only then when 'I am,'* E. P. Dutton, Triangle Editions (New York: 1978).

✛

POSTSCRIPT

The Works Of Love

S INCE THESE LECTURES were given in 1956, new contacts and a
wider experience have so enriched my understanding of the
Unitive Energy (E2) that I feel bound to restate my beliefs regarding the nature and role of this Cosmic Power.

The entire Creation is engaged in the transformation of
Energies, and we may suppose that behind this transformation
stands a Great Purpose that must be served. For the Creation as a
whole, and for all its parts, this Purpose, of which the Transcendental Energy is the first, direct instrument, must be inexorable,
to be achieved whatever may be the cost to all created worlds. It
must immeasurably surpass all human understanding. The naive
belief that the world was created for man has long since passed into
the realm of childish absurdity. We cannot conceive that the
entire human race can count for anything in a Purpose so tremendous as to require the creation of a hundred billion galaxies and so
prodigious in its complexity as to call for entities ranging in size
and duration from subatomic particles that exist for a million
millionth of a second to families of galaxies working out their
destiny in thousands of millions of years. In this immensity, life —
which occupies an intermediate position between the infini-
tesimal particles and the quasi-infinite totality — would have no
meaning, if there were not some Power as great as the universe
itself to mediate between life's puny strivings and the Inexorable

117

Purpose behind the Whole. This mediating Power can be expressed in our scheme as the Unitive Energy which has the properties needed for fulfilling the role of linking every part of Creation to the Whole.

By its all-pervasive quality, the Unitive Energy enters into our human experience as awareness of the Universal Love. In the notion of an Energy that is Universal and yet Personal, beyond all life and yet the Source of all Life, we find a key to grasping the basic unity of the religious aspirations and strivings by which, from time immemorial, mankind has been stirred. The notion of Unity is primary and irreducible. There can be no limitation and no qualification of unity. If there is a link between the Transcendent Energy and the material worlds it has brought into existence, that link must connect everything into a coherent structure. If it were otherwise, the Universe would fall apart and there would be no possible communication between the fragments. In a word, there can be no partial unity. Either all is atomic, unconnected, and therefore meaningless; or else all is connected, structured and meaningful. If the smallest thing makes sense, then everything must make sense.

The converse does not hold. There might conceivably be a meaning in the total universe — but no meaning in any of its parts. No simple analogy will adequately express this notion, but we could conceive the gas in a balloon as totally meaningful because it makes the system buoyant, and yet without meaning in respect of its separate molecular motions. We could imagine a universe built up from atoms in meaningless random motion, and yet having a significance and purpose when seen as a whole. Thus, we can suppose that the Transcendent Energy subordinates the total existing universe to the Supreme Purpose but does not bestow meaning on the parts. This latter role is performed by the Unitive Energy in such a way as to satisfy the purpose and yet preserve the meaning of the parts. To do this, the Unitive Energy must transfer meaning from the whole to the part, and also build up meaning from the part to the whole.

The question now arises whether there are diverse meanings or only one. Is the reconciling note of the Unitive Energy played always upon the same note, or is there a harmony of union which requires many tonalities for its perfection! I am convinced that the pluralistic answer to this question is the true one. The Unitive Energy can be compared to radiation that is always the same in nature, but can have many different wavelengths or frequencies. Even in our limited human experience we can witness the Unitive Energy at work on many different wavelengths. This brings me to the kernel of my theme in this postscript. There is a single energy that can be described as Universal Love, but it works in different ways and upon different levels. To understand better the nature of the Unitive Energy, we may refer to the Tetrad of Cosmic Energies, Transcendent, Unitive, Creative, and Conscious.

The two middle terms are distinguished by the inwardness of unity, and the outwardness of creativity. We can develop this notion intuitively for the Unitive Energy, by associating with it the characteristics of an all-pervasive reconciling and unifying Power. Characterized by total inwardness, it must enter everywhere and into everything. It can adapt itself equally to the very small and the very great. Space and Time, Size and Complexity place no restrictions upon its action. It can unify the prodigious complexity of an entire galaxy with its hundred thousand million stars into a supra-personal experience. It can awaken personal love in the heart of man. It can also embrace in its compassion the single sparrow that falls to the ground.

It is hard to resist the temptation to explore the theological implications of such a conception. Love that is Universal, Personal, able to embrace all Existence in the compassion, can be no other than the manifestation of Divine Love. We must not identify the Unitive Energy with God, for by hypothesis, it is within the Creation and subordinate to the Transcendent Purpose. Nevertheless, it seems to me that the notion merits the attention of theologians. The geocentric conception of the relationship between Man, God, and the World has been tacitly abandoned and must be replaced by a cosmic interpretation vast enough to accommodate our modern awareness of the unimaginable extent of the Creation and yet inward enough to preserve the personal and intimate character of our own experience of the Words of Love in the human soul. The failure to enunciate a conception of Love that will satisfy these two requirements is one of the principal causes of the divorce between religious and scientific cosmology. There is nothing illogical or "unscientific" in the conception of an Energy that is totally free from any of the limitations of existence and yet is contained within the Creation. We are living in a period when the call to union sounds more loudly than the objections of a timid conservation. We must broaden our conceptions, providing we can do so without imperilling the most precious element of religious experience — the conviction that there is a personal bond between God and the human soul.

A better understanding of the Unitive Energy may help us not only to the reconciliation of science and religion, but also to see a common Source of all religious experience. I have headed this postscript "The Works of Love." The plural indicates that though Love is One, its works are varied. A simple analogy is given by electo-magnetic radiation, which is everywhere the same in its nature but differs in its action according to its frequency and intensity. We should certainly picture to ourselves the Unitive Energy as One in Nature and diverse in Manifestation. Each "wavelength" will produce a specific "Work of Love." Every mode of religious experience, every kind of bond that draws men together in their search for deliverance from the separations of time and place, every human and indeed every animal sympathy can be regarded as a specific "wavelength." The mutual denials that have so afflicted men in their search for Unity have no more sense than if those who love "blue" were to deny that "yellow" is a colour. The converse is also true: that different wavelengths are not to be identified or confused. As it would be false to say that yellow and blue are identical, so would it be false to say that to be a Muslim is the same as to be a Christian. Each faith has its own characteristic "wavelength" bearing its own "programme," and need not deny the validity of others.

These general considerations acquire a very present and urgent significance for anyone who has entered into intimate contact with more than one religion or with more than one spiritual technique. In recent years, I have done both. I am convinced that there is One and only one Unitive Power — which is the Love of God. But I am also convinced that this Power manifests and works validly in different ways. There is convincing evidence, for anyone who has eyes to see, that the Unitive Energy works in cycles — sometimes more openly, sometimes more withdrawn. We are now entering a period of increasing activity. It is seen as a spiritualizing action that is renewing the life of all the great religions and touching individuals in special ways. Whatever form the action may take, it always has the characteristics I have associated with the Divine Love or Unitive Energy.

Nevertheless, I am bound to conclude that the very essence of the Unitive Energy lies in its **redemptive action**. The inexorable austerity of the Supreme Purpose can be mitigated only by an equally Supreme and equally Universal Power of Love. It seems to me that the Christian Faith and the Doctrine of the Incarnation and the Redemption of the World by God Incarnate most nearly and most fully express the central Unity in which all the Works of Love originate and find their consummation.

✤

Claymont Communications was established by the Claymont Society for Continuous Education, a non-profit organization, in 1978 to publish and distribute books, tapes, and related materials concerning transformation. A wide range of works by John G. Bennett and many other authors is offered. For more information, write to:

Claymont Communications
P. O. Box 112
Charles Town, West Virginia 25414

Those who wish to pursue these ideas further are invited to contact:

The Claymont Society
Rt. 1 Box 279
Charles Town, West Virginia 25414

or

Shantock Press
Shantock Hall
Bovingdon, Hertsfordshire
HP3 0NG England